PENGUIN BOOKS

IT AIN'T CHEATIN' IF YOU DON'T
GET CAUGHT

Dan Gutman has written two previous books—*The
Greatest Games* (1984) and *I Didn't Know You
Could Do THAT with a Computer!* (1986). He
writes a syndicated newspaper column (also titled
"I Didn't Know You Could Do THAT with a Com-
puter!") and his articles have appeared in *Success,
Discover, Psychology Today, New Woman, Science
Digest, USA Today,* and many other publications.
He lives in Haddonfield, New Jersey, with his wife,
Nina, and two cats, Scrumpy and Mookie.

DAN GUTMAN

Scuffing,

Corking, Spitting,

Gunking, Razzing, and Other

Fundamentals of Our

National Pastime

. . .

It
Ain't
Cheatin'
If You Don't Get
Caught

. . .

PENGUIN BOOKS

PENGUIN BOOKS
Published by the Penguin Group
Viking Penguin, a division of Penguin Books USA Inc.,
40 West 23rd Street, New York, New York 10010, U.S.A.
Penguin Books Ltd, 27 Wrights Lane,
London W8 5TZ, England
Penguin Books Australia Ltd, Ringwood,
Victoria, Australia
Penguin Books Canada Ltd, 2801 John Street,
Markham, Ontario, Canada L3R 1B4
Penguin Books (N.Z.) Ltd, 182–190 Wairau Road,
Auckland 10, New Zealand

Penguin Books Ltd, Registered Offices: Harmondsworth, Middlesex, England

First published in Penguin Books 1990

1   3   5   7   9   10   8   6   4   2

LIBRARY OF CONGRESS CATALOGING IN PUBLICATION DATA
Gutman, Dan.
It ain't cheatin' if you don't get caught: scuffing, corking, spitting,
gunking, razzing, and other fundamentals of our national pastime /
Dan Gutman.
    p.   cm.
Includes bibliographical references.
ISBN 0 14 01.1652 4
    1. Baseball—United States—History—Miscellanea.   2. Baseball—
United States—Corrupt practices.   I. Title.
GV863.A1G9   1990
796.357'0973—dc20   89-22836

Printed in the United States of America
Set in Linotron DeVinne
Designed by Kathryn Parise

For Adam, Nathan,
Rachel, Brian, and Samantha.

The fans of tomorrow.

"I try not to break the rules
but merely test their elasticity."
—Bill Veeck

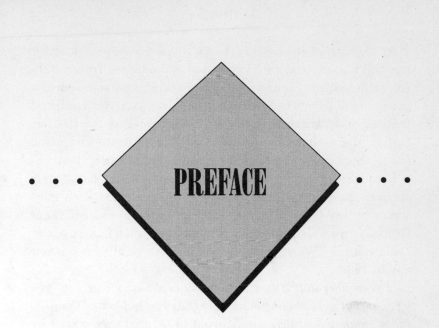

PREFACE

Where It All Didn't Begin

· · ·

I guess you could say cheating has been going on in baseball since the very beginning, because the first guy to cheat was Abner Doubleday.

Well, Doubleday didn't actually cheat at the game itself. He never even *played* baseball and wouldn't have known the difference between a shortstop and a backstop. Abner Doubleday never invented baseball—it was the other way around.

At the turn of the century, there was a debate over whether baseball was conceived in America or was adapted from a British game called "rounders." Former pitcher and sporting goods mogul Albert G. Spalding insisted the American national pastime was American-born. In 1906, he called for the formation of a national commission to settle the matter once and for all. Spalding appointed the commission himself.

Recollections and evidence poured in from old ballplayers all over the country, but the one letter that was taken most seriously was from a Denver mining engineer named Abner Graves. Graves claimed to be a playmate of a man named Abner Doubleday in Cooperstown, New York. He recalled a summer day in 1839:

"I remember well Abner Doubleday explaining 'base ball' to a lot of us that were playing marbles in the street in front of Cooper's tailor shop, and drawing a diagram in the dirt with a stick by marking out a square with a punch mark in each corner for bases, a ring in the centre for pitcher, a punch mark just back of home base for catcher, two punch marks for outfielders ..."

Graves, it should be noted, also claimed to have been one of the first Pony Express riders. In any case, Spalding was attracted to the patriotically romantic story, especially with Doubleday being a Civil War hero who had fought at Gettysburg and supposedly aimed the first gun at Fort Sumter. It didn't hurt that Doubleday—long dead—had once been a friend of A. G. Mills, chairman of Spalding's commission. Ignoring any other evidence, the commission approved the Graves story and the myth of Abner Doubleday was born.

Historians are now virtually positive that Doubleday had nothing to do with the birth of baseball. There are more than a few reasons:

• Doubleday didn't mention baseball once in the sixty-seven diaries he left behind.

• Doubleday wasn't *in* Cooperstown in 1839. He was a student at West Point. His family had moved from Cooperstown two years earlier.

• Doubleday and Mills were friends for thirty years, but Mills, a baseball man who became president of the National League, didn't hear about Doubleday inventing the game until long after Doubleday died.

• Doubleday was twenty years old in 1839. His ''playmate'' Abner Graves was five.

• Graves wasn't the most credible witness. He was judged to be criminally insane when, at age ninety, he shot and killed his wife, who was forty-two years younger. He died in a Pueblo, Colorado, asylum in 1926.

• There are many pre-1839 references to baseball. A 1744 London children's booklet describes a game called ''base-ball'' with this rhyme: *"The ball once struck off / Away flied the boy / To the next destined post / And then home with joy."*

Myths die hard. We all eventually have to face up to the fact that there is no Santa Claus, and if the truth be known, Tinker, Evers, and Chance hated each other's guts. The myth of Abner Doubleday scratching his new game in the dirt with a stick persists to this day. We still hear sportscasters say things like ''After that bonehead play, folks, Abner Doubleday must be turning over in his grave!'' Doubleday is baseball's Santa Claus.

So, as I said, cheating in baseball goes back a long way. Like Abner Doubleday, it will be with us forever.

• • • • ACKNOWLEDGMENT • • •

You wouldn't be holding this book in your hands if not for the help and support of many people. First of all, Paul Hoffman and Jeff Kluger of *Discover* magazine, who sparked the idea in the first place. At the National Baseball Hall of Fame and Museum Library: Tom Heitz, Bill Deane, Pat Kelly, and Gretchen Curtis. The helpful folks in the Brooklyn Public Library Periodicals Department. Chuck Stevens of the Association of Professional Ball Players of America. The players and other baseball people who consented to speak about this controversial subject. Harold Berlin, Steve Bloom, Dr. Peter Brancazio, Roger Devine, Ralph Hammelbacher, Alan Kors, Stuart Krichevsky, David Stanford, and Chuck Verrill. And, of course, Nina.

CONTENTS

• Contents •

· Contents ·

Illustrations follow pages 64 and 138.

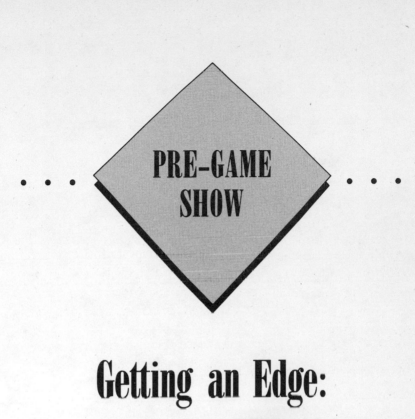

PRE-GAME
SHOW

Getting an Edge:

Why Cheating Is So Engrained
in Baseball

"The rule is, 'Do anything you can get away
with.'"

—Heywood Broun, 1923

This book isn't *only* about cheating. Call it cheating, call it gamesmanship, better yet call it *getting an edge*. This book is a celebration of all the things players, managers, owners, and even *fans* have done through the history of baseball to gain an edge for their team. It's about the search for an advantage, any advantage. If a few silly rules have to be bent or broken along the way, well, that's baseball.

Getting an edge doesn't always mean breaking the rules. Good outfielders learn early in their careers that on an easy fly ball with a runner tagging up, you move back a few steps and run *into* the ball as you catch it, letting your forward momentum carry you into the throw. Once that was a trick; today it's a fundamental.*

How far will a guy go to get an advantage? John McGraw, the legendary manager of the New York Giants, actually considered the possibility of amputating pitchers' fingers to make them throw better curveballs! McGraw had seen the bewildering breaks of Mordecai "Three Finger" Brown, who lost part of his index finger in a corn shredder accident as a child. (Such bewildering breaks that he won 239 games and made it to the Hall of Fame.)

As an experiment, McGraw had his pitchers try to duplicate Brown's curve by lifting one finger when they threw the ball. Fortunately, the new curve didn't break any more than the old ones. "It's lucky for you fellows that it doesn't," McGraw told his starters, "because if I thought it did, I'd have a surgeon out here tomorrow."

Baseball players have used their ingenuity to squeeze out every possible advantage over the years, exploiting the rules

---

* Similarly, an anonymous minor leaguer one day noticed he could get a better jump tagging up from third if he moved up the line into left field and took a running start before the ball was caught. In this case, the strategy was ruled illegal.

in marvelously inventive ways and using every trick short of dismemberment. There's nothing in the rule book that says a third baseman can't stand on his head and field his position upside down while whistling ''Swanee'' whenever there's a full count. But if there were some advantage to doing that, somebody would figure it out, try it, and the commissioner would have to rule on whether or not it was legal.

Sometimes it's a fine line that separates strategy from cheating. On several occasions it has been necessary to change the rules of baseball when ballplayers concocted schemes that were within the rules but not ''in the spirit of the game.'' For example, in the days when it was a ''do over'' if the umpire got hit by a thrown ball, savvy infielders would whip the ball at the ump's head if no other play could be made. Now, the ball remains in play.

• Michael ''King'' Kelly, a popular player/captain for the Boston Beaneaters in the 1880s, was sitting out a game when an opposing player lofted a lazy foul ball toward the dugout. Seeing that his catcher, Charlie Ganzel, had no chance of making the play, captain Kelly shouted, ''Kelly now catching for Boston!'' and stepped out of the dugout to snare the ball. In no time, a rule was put into effect banning substitutions in mid-play.

Kelly was also an expert at faking an injury while running the bases, then suddenly recovering and taking an extra base.

• The infield fly rule exists partly because baseball pioneer George Wright discovered a loophole in the rules. Wright noticed that because runners had to hold up on fly balls, an infielder could intentionally drop the fly ball, force the helpless runner out, and complete the doubleplay by throwing to first. This ''trap-ball trick,'' as the play was called, was deemed unsportsmanlike and the infield fly rule was created to prevent it. (Some infielders still do it occasionally on bunts.)

· Jackie Robinson's ingenuity forced another rule change in 1956. Robinson took advantage of the fact that a runner was out if hit by a batted ball. When running off first into an obvious double-play grounder, Jackie would deliberately run *into* the ball. He was out automatically, but the batter would get to first base and the Dodgers would stay out of the DP. Because of Robinson, the rule was amended so both hitter and runner are out.

As baseball continues to evolve, players are constantly devising new schemes. Since artificial turf was introduced, shortstops have discovered that from deep in the hole they can get throws to first a few milliseconds faster if they deliberately throw a low short hop off the carpet instead of the usual weak, arching toss. St. Louis superstar Ozzie Smith is generally credited with that inspiration.

A Game of Deception

Baseball, more than any other sport, is a game of trickery and deception. The pitcher tries to fool the batter. The catcher tries to fool the umpire. The infielder tries to fool the runner. (The agent tries to fool the owner.) The game isn't played by three-hundred-pound steroid gulpers, like football, or seven-foot pituitary freaks, like basketball. Baseball players, when you see them in person, are surprisingly regular-looking guys and must rely on their wits.

Because baseball is more of a thinking man's game, clever plays and gambits have become part of its appeal and beauty. The game naturally lends itself to trickery and we admire players who use their ingenuity to succeed.

For the most part, we're talking about cheating here. The cold fact is that today's players know that the fundamentals of baseball include not only hitting, fielding, and running but also corking, spitting, scuffing, tarring, popping greenies, throwing shineballs, slimeballs, sleazeballs, and some tricks you probably never even dreamed of. Every few years the commissioner's office goes on a crusade to rid the sport of scoundrels, but their slap-on-the-wrist punishments are an acknowledgment that cheating is as much a part of our national pastime as peanuts and Cracker Jacks. No other sport lends itself to rule bending so easily, or has such a rich tradition of it. If they suspended all the cheaters, we'd have to go to soccer games this summer.

Ben Johnson cheats in the Olympics and is hustled home, his career ruined and reputation disgraced. Two weeks later, Jay Howell cheats in the National League playoffs and essentially gets two days off while the media argue over whether or not the penalty was too harsh. In baseball, there's no disgrace in cheating. Just as we admire clever criminals who escape from prison, ballplayers who discover an illegal edge are admired. When apprehended, they're embarrassed only for getting caught, not for breaking the rules. There is no stigma attached to the name of a player who cheats his way to the top. Unlike the Olympics, which for so many years denied it had any problems, baseball freely admits that the sport—like civilized society itself—is crawling with bums.

From the days of John McGraw through those of Tug McGraw, the baseball establishment has been winking at cheating. Many admitted cheaters (most notably, Whitey Ford) are enshrined in the Hall of Fame, and there is no tarnish on their reputations or outcry to have them kicked out. We can't help but admire the resourcefulness grown men display in their efforts to succeed in the game they love. And now that the average salary is nearly half a million dollars a year, there is even more of an incentive to get that edge.

The fans are always going to love it. Cheating adds something to the game. The fan in the stands can't help but snicker when grown men are caught with cork in their bats or sandpaper in their gloves. Unlike football, where cheating generally means ramming your finger into a guy's earhole, there's something whimsical and audacious about baseball cheating. It's a victimless crime, tolerated and long remembered as a part of the game's tradition and folklore.

So I figure we may as well enjoy it. Cheating makes perfect sense, when you think about it. After all, what would you expect of a game in which three-fourths of the world is in foul territory?

TIMELINE OF RULES AND RULE BENDING

◇ ◇

1845 : New York surveyor Alexander Cartwright lays out the first diamond, sets up formal rules for the game of baseball.

1858 : Jim Creighton of the Brooklyn Niagras uses wrist snap to put intentional spin on the ball. Called strikes introduced.

1864 : Candy Cummings invents the curveball.

1865 : Eddie Cuthbert of Philadelphia Keystones steals the first base.

1866 : Dickey Pearce of Brooklyn Atlantics lays down the first bunt.

1868 : Pitchers forbidden to bend their elbows.

1872 : Curveball legalized. Pitchers allowed to snap the ball, but only with underhand motion.

1881 : Pitching box moved back five feet, now fifty feet from the batter.

• • •

TIMELINE OF RULES AND RULE BENDING

◇ ◇

• • • • • • • • • • • • • • • • • •

1882: Umpires instructed to stop soliciting views of players and spectators before making calls. National League ump Richard Higham expelled from baseball for consorting with gamblers. Pitching box moved back another five feet.

1884: Pitchers allowed to throw overhand with any motion.

1885: Bats with one side flattened are legalized. Pitchers prohibited from taking a running start before throwing the ball.

1886: Flat bats banned. National League founded.

1887: The last pitching restrictions are removed. Four strikes, yer out! Five balls, take your base.

1888: Three strikes, yer out!

1893: Distance from home plate to pitching rubber lengthened to sixty feet, six inches.

1895: Foul tips ruled strikes.

1897: Pitchers fined five dollars for intentionally damaging the ball.

1898: Balk rule instituted.

1901: Foul balls ruled strikes. American League founded.

1902: George Hildebrand invents the spitball.

• • •

TIMELINE OF RULES AND RULE BENDING

◇ ◇

• • • • • • • • • • • • • • • • •

1904: Pitching mound limited to fifteen inches in height.

1908: Bert Hall invents the forkball.

1910: Russell Ford invents the scuffball. Cork-centered ball introduced.

1920: Rules committee outlaws all pitches that result from tampering with the ball. Ray Chapman killed by pitched ball. Eight players of Chicago White Sox found to have thrown 1919 World Series. Federal Judge Kenesaw Mountain Landis elected first commissioner of baseball, bans the "Black Sox" for life. Runners prohibited from running the bases backward "for the purpose of confusing the infielders or making a travesty of the game."

1925: Pitchers allowed to dry their hands with a resin bag. Sam Rice controversy (see "The Forty-nine Year Putout," in Chapter 9).

1934: Burleigh Grimes throws the last legal spitball.

1938: Gaylord Perry born.

1939: Laminated bats banned.

1941: Mickey Owen drops third-strike spitter, allowing Yankees to win World Series.

1944: Nelson Potter of St. Louis ejected for throwing spitballs.

• • •

TIMELINE OF RULES AND RULE BENDING

◇ ◇

1951: Eddie Gaedel, a midget, bats in major league game. Midgets banned thereafter.

1962: Hitters may apply a substance to the bat, but no more than eighteen inches up the handle.

1964: Gaylord Perry throws his first spitball, in twenty-three-inning game.

1965: Gloves with a circumference of more than thirty-eight inches, which Hoyt Wilhelm's catchers had been using to catch his knuckleballs, are banned.

1968: Pitchers banned from going to their mouths with pitching hand while on the mound. If a pitcher does it when there is a baserunner, it's a balk. If there's no runner, it's a ball. "The Year of the Pitcher."

1969: Pitching mound lowered to ten inches.

1973: First spitball offense ruled a ball, the second means ejection. American League institutes designated hitter.

1974: Umpires may declare an illegal pitch without physical evidence. "Cupped" bats are ruled legal. Graig Nettles Super Ball incident.

1978: Don Sutton of Dodgers threatens to sue after being ejected for scuffing.

• • •

TIMELINE OF RULES AND RULE BENDING

◇ ◇

• • • • • • • • • • • • • • •

1980 : Rick Honeycutt caught on mound with thumb-tack stuck through a Band-Aid on his finger.

1982 : Gaylord Perry wins three-hundredth game, re-tires.

1983 : George Brett pine-tar incident.

1986 : Split-finger fastball popularized by Roger Craig.

1987 : "The Year of the Cheater." Kevin Gross, Joe Niekro, and Billy Hatcher suspended ten days each for scuffing and corking violations. Many other play-ers accused.

1988 : Jay Howell of Dodgers ejected and suspended for throwing pine-tar ball during National League playoffs.

1989 : Dennis Eckersley of Oakland Athletics accused of hiding an emery board in his glove, down his shirt, in his pocket, and down his pants during American League playoffs.

• • •

1st

INNING

The Early Days

"The game of baseball is a clean, straight game, and it summons to its presence everybody who enjoys clean, straight athletics."
— President William Howard Taft

The Worst Cheaters in Baseball

The dirtiest team in baseball history was the Baltimore Orioles of the 1890s. Led by John McGraw, Wilbert Robinson, "Wee Willie" Keeler, Hughie Jennings, and manager Ned Hanlon, they practiced an early form of "Billyball" taken to an extreme, especially during home games.

The Orioles blatantly tripped opposing runners and threw equipment in their way. On the basepaths, they slapped the ball out of the fielder's hands. Their idea of advancing the runner was to dive into the first baseman after he caught the ball. A decade or more before the era of Ty Cobb, the Orioles filed their spikes until they cut like razors.

In those days there was usually only one umpire officiating the game, and the Orioles perfected the art of running from first to third base without touching second. Other teams quickly picked up on this, and in *The Glory of Their Times* Sam Crawford tells the story of Cincinnati runner Jake Beckley, who went directly from second base to the plate without touching third. After Beckley slid home safely in a cloud of dust, umpire Tim Hurst called him out.

"What do you mean, I'm out?" Beckley roared, outraged. "They didn't even make a play on me."

"You big S.O.B.," replied Hurst. "You got here *too* quick!"*

The fans weren't allowed to keep foul balls at the time, and

---

* Tim Hurst used to tell a story about what it was like to umpire a game in the days of the old Orioles. Christy Mathewson relates it in his book *Pitching in a Pinch*:

"The man started to steal," said Tim, "and as he left the bag he spiked the first baseman, who tried to trip him. The second baseman blocked the runner, and in sliding into the bag, the latter tried to spike Hugh Jennings, who was playing shortstop and covering, while Jennings sat on him to knock the wind out. The batter hit Wilbert Robinson, who was catching, on the hands with his bat so that he couldn't throw, and Robbie trod on my toes with his spikes and shoved his glove into my face so I couldn't see to give the decision. It was one of the hardest decisions that I have ever been called upon to make."

when the other team hit one into the stands an Oriole ringer would toss a beat-up, mushy ball that couldn't be hit out of the infield.

The Orioles' most devious trick was to stash a few extra balls strategically in the high outfield grass. When the opposing batter hit a long drive in the gap, Oriole outfielders would ignore the batted ball and simply pick up one of the hidden balls and throw it in, holding the confused hitter to a single.

On at least one occasion this trick backfired. In a game against the St. Louis Browns, Joe Quinn was on first when Tommy Dowd hit one to left center. Oriole left fielder Joe Kelley scooped up a hidden ball and fired out Quinn at third. Unfortunately, as this was happening, centerfielder Steve Brodie was still chasing down the game ball and threw that one in, *too*. When the dust had settled and the arguments were over, the umpire forfeited the game to St. Louis.

John McGraw, who played third on this team, was particularly shameless in his desire to win at all costs. "He uses every low and contemptible method that his erratic brain can conceive to win a play by a dirty trick," said National League President John Heydler of McGraw.

McGraw's most famous trick was to grab the runner's belt as he was getting set to tag up on a fly ball. When the runner took off, he'd go nowhere. Again, this was a trick that usually worked, but not always. Louisville's Pete Browning, who had fallen for the ploy before, got back at McGraw one day. When the batter hit the ball, Browning unfastened his belt buckle. The catch was made and Browning took off for home holding his pants up, while McGraw stood there with nothing but Browning's belt in his hands.

McGraw would also egg on the drunken fans, who would bring small mirrors to the ballpark and flash them into the

---

"What did you do?" I asked him.

"I punched Robbie in the ribs, called it a foul, and sent the runner back," replied Tim.

other team's eyes at appropriate moments—such as while they were hovering under fly balls.

Even the Baltimore groundskeeper Tom Murphy got into the act. He would mix chips of soap into the dirt around the pitcher's box so opposing hurlers would get their hands slippery and lose their grip on the ball. (The spitball had not yet been invented.) The Oriole pitchers knew where to reach to get fresh dirt.

In those days the ground crew's shack was in fair territory. One time an Oriole batter lined a ball into the shack and the quick-thinking crew slammed the door shut so the left fielder couldn't get in.

But the old Orioles weren't just hoodlums, as was often claimed. They were defining baseball fundamentals for future generations. They realized they had to *know* the rules in order to bend them, and developed many of the techniques that are now standard baseball strategy. Baltimore is credited with having invented the hit-and-run, the sacrifice bunt, the squeeze play, the cut-off man, and the double steal. They were the first team to intentionally walk a batter to set up a possible double play.

The "Baltimore chop" got its name from this team, when they found they could swing down at the ball and bounce it so high that the hitter made it to first easily. When their opponents had runners on second and third, catcher Wilbert Robinson devised "the old sucker throw." He'd fake a pickoff to second and catch the runner at third leaning the wrong way.

All these "tricks" made up what came to be called "inside baseball," and it dominated the game until Babe Ruth and the home-run era came along twenty-five years later.

The Orioles played dirty, but it should be noted that baseball was in its infancy at the time. Whenever a new sport is born, the line between cheating and fair play is fuzzy simply because the rules are still evolving. In the early days of baseball, the number of strikes necessary for an out or balls necessary for a walk changed almost yearly. For eight years after the curveball was invented, it was illegal. The spitball, on the other hand, was perfectly legal when invented and only banned sixteen years later. The men who played the game before the turn of the century probably had a tough time even knowing what the rules *were,* much less abiding by them.

The rules of the game are still evolving to this day, though most fans like to think baseball is an unchanging throwback to the past. The introduction of artificial surfaces and the designated hitter in the American League are radical changes in the way the game is played. There have also been experiments (almost always to help the struggling hitters) to test the effects of livelier balls, "automatic" intentional walks, changing the strike zone, and lowering the mound. In 1970, the Gulf Coast rookie league tested the effect of bending the foul lines three degrees outward once they passed first and third base, a change which creates 2,771 more feet of fair territory on a baseball field. Like most young prospects, the plan never made it to the big leagues.

The legacy of the old Baltimore Orioles has been passed down through the baseball generations over the last one hundred years. Many of the players on the team went on to become managers themselves. The most successful was McGraw, who won ten pennants with the New York Giants and drummed his lessons into a (believe-it-or-not) young outfielder named Casey Stengel. When he became a manager himself, Stengel led his Yankees to another ten pennants and passed along the wisdom to his second baseman and surrogate son Billy Martin. And so it goes.

The "Gentleman's Game"

When Alexander Cartwright (not Abner Doubleday) had the genius to lay out the diamond in such a way as to make an infield ground ball reach first base nearly at the same instant as a hustling runner, baseball was a leisure game for the upper classes. Professional gentlemen gathered on mid-week afternoons for matches, and both teams would attend a banquet or ball afterward. Expenses were paid by club membership dues. The idea of a player being paid to play was beyond comprehension. It's doubtful that anyone would have bothered cheating to win a ballgame, as it was more of a social occasion than a competition.

The rise of the railroad and the American Civil War served to spread baseball around the country, as well as to all social classes. Soon hundreds of towns had their own teams, and having a good one became a source of pride in the community. Winning became important, and big, athletic men, even if they were from the lower classes, were suddenly being recruited to join baseball teams.

By 1858, admission was being charged for games, and in 1860 scandal erupted when the Brooklyn Excelsiors had the audacity to actually *pay* a man to play. Baseball history books usually name James Creighton as the first to play baseball for money. The Cincinnati Red Stockings of 1869 were the first team to actually announce salaries ($600–$2,000 for a season) and manager Harry Wright spent $15,000 to lure the best players in the country to play for the team. Albert Spalding was one of the stars of that team, and one of the first to see baseball as his career. "I had determined to enter Baseball as a profession," he wrote. "I was neither ashamed of the game nor of my attachment to it."

The Red Stockings even turned a profit that year—$1.26.

Baseball was becoming more popular and gradually was transformed from a leisure pastime to a business. "Dominant American values, such as fierce competition and creeping commercialism, disrupted the climate of sportsmanship," wrote David Quentin Voigt in *American Baseball,* his two-volume history of the sport. To some purists, professionalism was the end of baseball "like it oughta be."

The Players

Before Jim Bouton's *Ball Four,* most fans seemed to think that baseball players were baby-faced, squeaky clean, all-American boys who cared about nothing more than upholding American values. In fact, up until recent decades many players were illiterate, intoxicated louts who spent their time at pool halls, saloons, and with bookmakers when they weren't on the diamond. More than a few players were charged with murder. Stories of homeless has-been stars of the 1880s were common, as was suicide. Hall of Famer Ed Delahanty jumped off a bridge to his death.

There were no beer commercials in those days, but today's advertising execs certainly would have signed up "Smiling Mickey" Welch, who claimed that drinking beer was the reason he was such a good pitcher. He even wrote his own slogan: "Pure elixir of malt and hops, beats all the drugs and all the drops." Mike "King" Kelly, the Boston Beaneaters' captain, wouldn't have made as effective a corporate spokesperson—he drank himself to death. At least the old-time ballplayers weren't accused—as are the players of today—of lacking color.

It's often said that the old-time player was tougher—that he would shake off injuries that put the modern player on the disabled list. True, but it should be mentioned that when players had to sit out games in the early days, their paltry paychecks were cut off immediately and they were out of jobs until they recovered.

For a time, the game was played without gloves, and to avoid hurting their hands players used the "cap catch"—they'd take their caps off and snare fly balls in them. That was quickly ruled illegal. When protective gear was introduced, the men who used it were accused of being cowards and hypochondriacs. James Tyng, the first player to wear a catcher's mask, was ridiculed unmercifully by both players and fans.

o

It was no picnic to be a fan—or what was called a "krank"—in those days. Pickpockets roamed the crowd freely. On one occasion, somebody set up a phony gate, charged people to get into the ballfield, and pocketed all the money. To please the crowd, many teams hired Negro mascots, though non-whites were not allowed to actually play the game. Less crowd-pleasing was the policy that fans were required to throw back foul balls—Braves' owner George Grant would actually climb into the stands and snatch balls away from fans who wanted to take home a souvenir.

Baseball was hopelessly corrupt. Players were quick to jump their contracts for a better offer, and strong teams raided the weaker teams at will. The National League was formed in 1876 to correct these and other abuses, but as the game became more of an organized business, a new element came in—professional gamblers.

Gambling was considered to be a symbol of gentility in those times, certainly more than playing baseball was. As early as the 1880s, gamblers were working the stands giving odds and taking bets from fans and even from players. The practice of fixing games and making them out to be legitimate was called "hippodroming." When World War I began, racetracks were closed by the government and gamblers switched their interest to baseball.

The Black Sox Scandal, in which eight members of the 1919 Chicago White Sox threw the World Series, was the most notorious gambling incident in baseball's history, but certainly not the only one. In 1877 four Louisville players were banned for life for fixing games. Their techniques involved sending telegrams with the word "SASH" to indicate a fix was on ("sure as shit"). Cincinnati star Hal Chase was nabbed fixing his own games, and after being suspended he had the nerve to sue the team for back pay. (Even more remarkable, he was reinstated!)

A group of players who had been blacklisted formed their

own barnstorming team called "The Blacklisted" and were so successful that the league allowed them back in. At one point, teams were prohibited from announcing the next day's starting pitchers for fear that gamblers would get to them.

Even the great Ty Cobb was accused of arranging a one-game fix to help Detroit gain third place in 1919. When word got out, Cobb threatened to sue baseball and expose its corruption. He was allowed to finish his career honorably.

When I say gambling, I don't mean polite office betting pools. In his book *Eight Men Out*, Eliot Asinof described what a day at the ballpark was like:

"An outfielder, settling under a crucial fly ball, would find himself stoned by a nearby spectator, who might win a few hundred dollars if the ball was dropped. On one occasion, a gambler actually ran out on the field and tackled a ballplayer. On another, a marksman prevented a fielder from chasing a long hit by peppering the ground around his feet with bullets."

The recent scandal involving Pete Rose shows that modern-day baseball is not invulnerable to gambling. Leo Durocher was suspended for a year for consorting with gamblers in 1947, and Philadelphia owner William D. Cox was permanently suspended in 1943 for betting on Phillies games. In 1960, American League umpires Ed Runge and Bill McKinley were approached by men offering bribes. After making a controversial interference call against Boston during the 1975 World Series, umpire Larry Barnett received a letter from a bettor demanding that he pay ten thousand dollars or get a ".38 caliber bullet in your head" if the Red Sox lost.

It should come as no surprise that the first men to play baseball for a living were considered to be human scum, on a level with men who chose acting as a profession. (In fact, many early ballplayers took on acting jobs during the off-season.) Sports in general were looked down upon in the 1800s, and baseball in particular. *The New York Times* reported in the 1870s that a ballplayer was a ''shiftless member of the laboring class, prone to drink, having a loose moral code and preferring to avoid an honest day's work by playing ball.'' The paper also informed its readers that baseball was the cause of 37,518 accidents, including 1,900 instances of eyes being poked out.

You didn't take a girl to a ballgame. Priests were forbidden to attend games, and religious groups went so far as to disrupt streetcar lines to prevent the sport from being played on Sundays. If a game *did* take place on the day of rest, police would march on the field and arrest all the players. Robert Downing, the second baseman of the Chicago White Sox, changed his name so his minister father wouldn't know he played baseball.

President Benjamin Harrison made it a point not to be seen at a game. When his daughter married a ballplayer, Abraham Lincoln's son Robert Todd Lincoln referred to the young man as a ''baseball buffoon.'' People who lived near ballfields argued that their property values were lowered. No self-respecting hotel would let a team of ballplayers stay there. When teams went out for dinner and ordered steaks, the waiters would yell, ''Baseball steak!'' indicating that the chef should bring out the worst cuts available.

''Baseball was mighty glamorous and exciting to me,'' wrote Connie Mack years later, ''but there is no use in blinking at the fact that at that time the game was thought, by solid respectable people, to be only one degree above grand larceny, arson and mayhem, and those who engaged in it were beneath the notice of decent society.''

The integrity of the game, if there was any, rested on the shoulders of the unfortunate men who chose careers as umpires. If the ballplayers had it bad, the umpires had it worse. They were considered to be evil, cowardly, and were hated by all. Occasionally an umpire was cheered—usually after taking a foul tip in the groin. A popular poem of the day went:

Mother, may I slug the umpire,
May I slug him right away,
So he cannot be here, mother,
When the clubs begin to play?
Let me clasp his throat, dear mother,
In a dear, delightful grip,
With one hand, and with the other
Bat him several in the lip.

If you've ever wondered why they don't allow cans and bottles into ballparks, it's because paper cups don't hurt as much when they bounce off an umpire's head. In 1907, umpire Billy Evans's skull was fractured by a bottle thrown out of the stands. We scream "Kill the umpire!" in jest, but in 1899 an angry player disputed a call by slamming his bat at the head of minor league umpire Samuel White, killing him. Another ump, Harry Pulliam, committed suicide.

"The mortality in umpires was high," wrote Connie Mack. "We seemed to use them up pretty fast."

With the unsavory characters, cheating, gambling, booze, and corruption, baseball may have reflected turn-of-the-century America perfectly, but was hardly the example for the nation's youth. Five years after the National League was founded, *The New York Times* claimed, "There is reason to believe that base ball is gradually dying out in this country."

Almost from the beginning, the powers-that-be in baseball became obsessed with the idea that the game needed to project an uplifting, moral image. "Ladies' day" games were held, with the belief that women in the ballpark would make the men behave more respectably. Box seats were installed to cultivate a higher-class crowd. Opposing dugouts were separated to reduce confrontations between teams.

It was considered crucial to the survival of baseball to present a favorable image, to paint a picture of a sport in which nobody cheats, gambles, or drinks, and ballparks are clean, safe sanctuaries where respectable people can enjoy healthy athletic competition. This remarkably successful snow job held up pretty well until *Ball Four*. For the most part, America has ignored the reality, bought the image, and anointed the game as its national pastime.

Even today, the most challenging task of the commissioner of baseball is to protect the game's positive image. Baseball players are held up to a higher moral standard than just about any other profession. Most teams maintain curfews and bedchecks, treating their men like boys. For the sake of the game's image, players are told when they have to wear a tie and whether or not they can grow a beard.

Imagine—guys are making a million dollars a year, yet they can't determine their own bedtime or pick out their own clothes in the morning! The dichotomy between baseball's image and baseball's reality may be one reason why incidents of cheating seem to take on so much significance when they occur. It's like the wicked delight we get upon hearing that Miss America posed for nude pictures or was caught shoplifting.

Eventually, the game of baseball did become respectable, but it wasn't because of box seats or players wearing neckties. What really cleaned up the game were heroic figures like Christy Mathewson, Connie Mack, Ban Johnson, and Judge Kenesaw Mountain Landis.

Mathewson was an all-American college boy who served as class president at Bucknell and was a member of its glee club and literary society before becoming the star pitcher of the New York Giants. Though he was sometimes referred to as a sissy in the ballpark and the papers, most Americans had in Mathewson their first baseball hero. Oddly enough, he was a roommate and lifelong friend of the man whose image was completely opposite his own, John McGraw.

On the managing side, Cornelius McGillicuddy (Connie

Mack) brought decency to the game. "There is room for gentlemen in any profession," he claimed. "I will not tolerate profanity, obscene language or personal insults from my bench. . . . I always will insist as long as I am manager of the club that my boys be gentlemen." As it turned out, he was manager for fifty-three years, wearing his suit and hat in the dugout well into his eighties.

Even Connie Mack was no saint when it came to cheating. In a *Saturday Evening Post* article, he described a little trick from his catching days, when a caught foul tip was counted as an out:

"One day I got an idea. When the batter swung at a ball and missed it, I slapped the tip of my mitt with the fingers of my right hand . . . making a sound exactly as if the batter had touched the ball. . . . I fooled the umpire time after time with this little deception. In most cases the batter himself heard the sound of my fingers on the mitt and thought his bat had kissed the ball."

The other driving force in making baseball respectable was Byron Bancroft "Ban" Johnson. As president of the Western League in the 1890s, he fought against rowdyism, gamblers, and drunkenness. Liquor was not sold in his ballparks. Fines and suspensions were levied for umpire-baiting. Humorless and dictatorial, Johnson was once described as "a man who looked as though he might have been weaned on an icicle." Still, his contribution to the game was huge—he founded the American League in 1901.

Unfortunately, the Black Sox Scandal pretty much wiped out any respectability these three brought to the sport and it became necessary to set even stricter limits if baseball was to survive. In 1920, the panicky team owners called in tough Chicago federal judge Kenesaw Mountain Landis, son of a Union Army surgeon who lost his leg at the Battle of Kennesaw Mountain. He was named commissioner for life and given total authority. "Get that old guy who sits behind first base all the time," cracked Will Rogers. "He's out there every day anyhow!" (Seven years later, Hollywood made a similar move to clean up its act in appointing Will Hays as its czar.)

Landis didn't just clean up the game's image, he cleaned up the game. The Black Sox were booted out of baseball for life—even Buck Weaver, whose only crime was not ratting on his teammates. It was the intention of Landis to send a message to players and fans that from that day on, the game would command respect.

Nineteen-twenty was a turning point in baseball history. Besides the exposure of the Black Sox Scandal and the appointment of Judge Landis, this was the year Cleveland shortstop Ray Chapman was killed when hit in the head by a pitched ball, the only recorded occurrence in a hundred and fifty years of major league baseball. This was the year twenty-five-year-old Babe Ruth slammed an unheard-of fifty-four home runs, putting an end to "inside baseball" and "the scientific style," and ushering in both the Roaring Twenties and the Home-Run Era.

Also new in 1920 was this little thing called Rule 8:02, which may have done more than anything else to "clean up" and revolutionize the game. As it reads today, the rule states:

The pitcher shall not—
(1) Bring his pitching hand in contact with his mouth or lips while in the 18-foot circle surrounding the pitching rubber;
(2) Apply a foreign substance of any kind to the ball;
(3) Expectorate on the ball, either hand or his glove;
(4) Rub the ball on his glove, person, or clothing;
(5) Deface the ball in any manner;
(6) Deliver what is called the "shine" ball, "spit" ball, "mud" ball or "emery" ball.

◇ **THEY SAID IT** ◇

· · · · · · · · · · · · · · · · · · · ·

"When I began playing the game, baseball was as gentlemanly as a kick in the crotch."

—*Ty Cobb*

"Many fans look upon an umpire as a sort of necessary evil to the luxury of baseball, like the odor that follows an automobile."

—*Christy Mathewson*

"There was a time when the National League stood for integrity and fair dealing; today it stands for dollars and cents."

—*John Montgomery Ward, in 1889*

"Cheating is baseball's oldest profession."

—Inside Sports

· · ·

The Spitball

"It's a hard slider."

—Five-year-old Allison Perry, when asked if her dad, Gaylord, throws a spitball.

Ah, the spitball. The damp delivery. The drugstore drop. Far more classic than Coke, the spitter is a piece of nostalgic Americana. A persecuted pitch, it was caught in the dragnet that ran the mudball, the scuffball, and all those other unsavory characters out of the game. But this bad boy of baseball had a special quality. It was so elegant in its simplicity, so mysterious, so devilishly clever. So damned hard to hit.

When the baseball rules committee was to meet on February 9, 1920, *The New York Times* reported : ''No radical departures from the present rules are looked for, but there is no telling what may develop when committees gather.''

No kidding. The next day, the spitball was outlawed and baseball was never the same.

Most fans think the introduction of a livelier, ''juiced-up'' ball in 1920 kicked off the modern era, and transformed baseball from a pitching and defensive game to an offensive, home run-oriented game. According to baseball authority Bill James, this is a myth. ''There was no lively ball,'' claims James. ''The same ball that was used in 1920 was used in 1919. I'm absolutely positive of that. It was just the banning of the spitball and balls that had been tampered with.''

Before the spitball and other trick pitches were outlawed, hitters hardly ever saw a clean white baseball. It was a rare game in which more than three baseballs were used. ''Heck, like I said, we'd play a whole game with one ball, if it stayed in the park,'' Sam Crawford told Lawrence Ritter in *The Glory of Their Times*. When a new ball was thrown in, the team in the field would immediately throw it around the horn and smear it with spit, mud, tobacco juice, or whatever else was handy.

A ball on its way to the plate was difficult to see, worn, and sometimes even lopsided. Some people believe Ray Chapman's death was a result of his inability to pick up the path of the dirty, sidearmed baseball hurtling at his head.

Dirty baseballs don't lend themselves to home runs, either. "Trick" pitches such as the spitball and scuffball usually break sharply downward, leading to ground balls and strikeouts. When you *did* hit a beat-up ball in the air, it didn't travel very far and players knew better than to *try* to hit it out of the park. Banning the spitter and putting clean balls in the game served to provide hitters with better visibility, pitches that didn't sink unnaturally, and balls that could be hit harder. This is what changed baseball from a strategic, low-scoring pitcher's game to an explosive hitting game.

Spitballs and highballs were banned within a year of each other, but rule 8:02 had about as much of an effect on illegal pitching as Prohibition had on drinking. Trick pitches, like booze, were merely driven underground. The spitter continues to be studied today, carefully taught in bullpens, and used during games, especially when a pitcher is in a tight spot and needs that inning-ending out. Estimates of the number of major league pitchers who doctor the ball in some way range anywhere from 10 to 50 percent.

And like anything else that is forbidden, it becomes more intriguing. Much of the appeal of illegal pitching today is the clever deception involved in hiding it, faking it, psyching opponents into thinking you're throwing it, and getting away with something that you're not allowed to do. The spitball is baseball moonshine.

How to Throw a Spitter

If you're going to break the rules, you might as well break them correctly. Branch Rickey once said he could teach anybody how to throw a spitball in fifteen minutes. I'll try not to keep you that long.

Every spitball pitcher throws the pitch differently, but all will agree that the idea is to throw the ball with little or no spin, like a knuckleball. A dab of saliva between your fingers and the ball will minimize friction and prevent the ball from rotating, as it usually does when we throw an object. A big glob is considered gauche. A little dab'll do ya. Say, just enough saliva to turn this page.

Grip the ball with your two first fingers on the top and your thumb on the bottom just as you would a fastball, but not on the seams. Seams make the ball spin. Your top two fingers should be wet, the thumb dry. Hold your wrist as rigid as you possibly can. As you release the ball, squirt it out of your fingers as if you were shooting a watermelon seed or pinching a Ping-Pong ball. Control takes a lot of practice.

A properly thrown spitter comes to the plate like any other pitch; then it suddenly looks like it gets tired and has announced its retirement in mid-flight. It should drop like it rolled off a table. When you get good, you may try putting your thumb on the lower seam to give the ball a little topspin. That will make it drop even more than a dead fish knuckleball. Don't try throwing your spitter on a rainy day—it's useless.

Going to your mouth is the simplest way to load up a spitball, but creativity is a much admired trait in baseball. Pitchers have gone out to the mound with crushed bananas in their pockets. Ross Grimsley kept a vial of liquid in his cap. Jim "Mudcat" Grant used to rub a bar of soap against his uniform for a half an hour before the game. Then when he'd wipe the sweat off, he'd load up. Grant was never caught, but said that on one very hot day his shirt started bubbling.

John Wyatt, a pitcher with the Kansas City As, used to hide a syringe filled with Vaseline in the thumb of his glove. After that trick was exposed, Wyatt came to the mound with a whole tube of Vaseline in his *mouth* and he squeezed out however much he needed using his teeth.

Jay Howell, who was ejected during the 1988 playoffs, wasn't the first to try the old pine-tar trick. Bob Moose was nabbed throwing a pine-tar ball in 1968, though his only penalty was a trip to the clubhouse to wash his hands. Paul Lindblad used to keep a pine-tar rag right in his glove. Vida Blue was once forced to change his pants in the middle of a game when umpire Greg Kosc discovered a spot of pine tar covered with resin. Blue explained that he must have bumped into somebody.

Clyde King never went in much for subtlety. When he pitched for the Dodgers, he once stuck a wad of bubble gum on the ball and zipped it past Whitey Lockman for a big strike-out. Of this peculiar trick, King said, ''The most important thing in throwing that pitch is to make sure the gum doesn't stick to your hand as you release it.''

There are a million ways to avoid getting caught throwing your spitter. You can hide your goo on the stripe of your uniform, behind an ear, under your cap, in your armpit, or in *all* those places. Develop a lot of interesting nervous twitches so hitters and umpires never know when you're going to throw a wet one. A good time to load up is during long foul balls. While everyone's watching the possible home run, you could mix up a batch of guacamole and put it on the ball without anyone noticing.

Or have your teammates load the ball for you. When Rusty Staub played first base for Houston, he spit on the ball while talking on the mound with pitcher Larry Dierker. The umpires called an automatic ball on Dierker. Nellie Fox, who played second base for the White Sox, was once thrown out of a game for putting tobacco juice on the ball. He is probably the only non-pitcher in baseball history to be ejected because of the spitball rule.

One thing to remember is to keep your stash in the dugout when you're not using it. In 1968 Phil Regan of the Cubs, frequently accused of being a spitballer, slid into second base wearing his warmup jacket. When he got up, umpires found a tube of Vaseline in the middle of the basepath. ''I never saw it before in my life,'' Regan claimed.

Incredibly, that incident resulted in no fines, no penalties, and not even a warning. Umpires see the spitters flying, but claim it's virtually impossible to prove that a man is wetting the ball. Since the spitter was banned seventy years ago, only two pitchers have been caught wet-handed and ejected from the game: Nelson Potter in 1944 and Gaylord Perry in 1982. Throwing a spitter is the baseball equivalent of jaywalking.

Umpires don't like the burden of being policemen. During a game in Boston some years back, umpire Hank Soar grew weary of complaints about spitters by the visiting team. Soar examined the ball, spit on it himself, and threw it back to the mound. If there was one umpire who was good at recognizing an illegal pitch, it was Bill Kunkel. He once admitted that when he was pitching for Kansas City, he'd thrown a pretty decent spitter himself.

The situation is so casually enforced that you barely have to hide your spitter in the major leagues. In fact, George Bamberger always believed that the best deception was no deception at all. "Just spit on your hand when they're looking at you," Bamberger said. "I never did it any other way."

Americans are obsessed with crime and criminals. Only a few men have ever confessed to throwing spitballs—Gaylord Perry, Preacher Roe, Whitey Ford, and a few others—but accusations abound. In researching this book, reading hundreds of books, magazines, and newspaper articles, I put together the following list of anyone and everyone who has been accused, justly or unjustly, of throwing spitballs in the major leagues.

NAMING NAMES:
ACCUSED OF THROWING SPITTERS

Glen Abbott	Stan Bahnsen
Jack Aker	Jack Baldschun
Johnny Allen	George Bamberger
Jim Bagby	Steve Barber

Jim Barr	Marv Grissom
Red Barrett	Dave Goltz
Gene Bearden	Lefty Gomez
Bo Belinsky	Jack Hamilton
Joe Black	Larry Jansen
Vida Blue	Ferguson Jenkins
Hank Borowy	Tommy John
Harry Brecheen	Matt Keough
Tommy Bridges	Ellis Kinder
Jim Brosnan	Clay Kirby
Bob Bruce	Ron Kline
Jim Bunning	Cal Koonce
Mike Caldwell	Bill Kunkel
Bill Castro	Rick Langford
Hugh Casey	Bill Lee
Dean Chance	Bob Lemon
Tony Cloninger	Dennis Leonard
Joe Coleman	Bob Locker
Doug Corbett	Billy Loes
Roger Craig	Jim Lonborg
Dave Danforth	Eddie Lopat
Murry Dickson	Steve McCatty
Bill Doak	Roger McDowell
Don Drysdale	Jim McGlothlin
George Earnshaw	Denny McLain
Dennis Eckersley	Don McMahon
Doc Ellis	Dave McNally
Dick Farrell	Sal Maglie
Whitey Ford	Jim Maloney
Art Fowler	Mike Marshall
Fred Frankhouse	Morrie Martin
George Frazier	Jim Merrill
Dave Freisleben	Ray Moore
Bob Friend	Bob Moose
Jim ''Mudcat'' Grant	George Munger
Ross Grimsley	Bob Newsom

Phil Niekro
Mike Norris
Blue Moon Odom
Dan Osinki
Joe Page
Claude Passeau
Orlando Pena
Ron Perranoski
Juan Pizarro
Nelson Potter
Bob Purkey
Pedro Ramos
Arthur "Bugs" Raymond
Phil Regan
Steve Rogers
Enrique Romo
Schoolboy Rowe
Bob Sadowski
Raul Sanchez
Fred Scherman
Calvin Schiraldi
Dave Schmidt
Johnny Schmitz

Jim Scott
Bob Shaw
Larry Sherry
Eric Show
Bil Singer
Paul Splittorff
Bob Stanley
Max Surkont
Bruce Sutter
Don Sutton
Ralph Terry
Thad Tillotson
Mike Torrez
Virgil Trucks
Bob Turley
Pete Vuckovich
Bob Welch
Stan Williams
Smokey Joe Williams
Earl Wilson
Jim Wilson
John Wyatt

The Spitball Hall of Fame

But those guys are lightweights. There are also those immortals who used their talent, determination, and various foreign substances to achieve a special place in baseball history. These men truly deserve the honor of being the first inductees into the Spitball Hall of Fame...

Gaylord "the King of Grease" Perry: The Babe Ruth of the spitball and the real symbol of competitive baseball gamesmanship. A simple peanut farmer from North Carolina, Perry pursued the ultimate spitter for twenty-two years, like Edison searching for the perfect filament for his incandescent bulb. He admitted using everything on the ball from baby oil and axle grease to suntan lotion and fishing-line wax. He was also master of the "powder-puff ball," which was coated with Pillsbury flour mix and came to the plate in a distracting white cloud.

"I reckon I tried everything on the old apple but salt and pepper and chocolate sauce toppin'," the colorful Perry said in his spit-and-tell autobiography *Me and the Spitter,* which he had the nerve to publish before he retired from the game.

Even before the book came out, everyone knew Perry (sometimes called "the Great Expectorator") threw the spitter and tried to catch him in the act. He was routinely frisked on the mound, toweled off, and forced to change his clothes in the middle of games. American League president Joe Cronin once had a chemist analyze baseballs thrown by Perry.

In 1973, the Yankees kept a pitching chart for one of Perry's games. Hitters claimed he threw thirty spitters, and when videotape of the game was reviewed, it revealed that Perry tugged the inside of his left sleeve with his right hand before each of those thirty pitches.

It didn't matter—Gaylord wasn't ejected from a game for throwing a spitball until he was forty-three years old. In a 1982 game against the Red Sox, umpire Dave Phillips decided he'd had enough and threw Perry out. The dues—two hundred and fifty dollars and a ten-day suspension. Not a bad price to pay for a brilliant career.

Perry and his spitter are a vast source of great baseball stories. Billy Martin (who claimed that Perry smelled like a drugstore) once brought a bloodhound to the ballpark on a day Perry was starting, to sniff out any foreign substances. Martin planned to have the dog sit next to him on the bench, but claimed the dog had a heart attack when it got a whiff of Gaylord. In 1981, a senior umpire told Perry to be out at the ballpark the next day at seven o'clock in the morning. The ump showed up with his son, and demanded that Perry show the boy how to throw a spitter.

Gaylord's spitter not only drove opponents crazy (Bobby Murcer sent him a gallon of lard as a gift), but his own teammates as well. Bobby Bonds once claimed that he dropped an outfield fly because it was so loaded with Perry's glop.

He must have been doing something right. Perry is the only man to have won the Cy Young award in both leagues (1972 and 1978), one of them at the age of forty. He won 314 games lifetime (including a no-hitter), and received 304 votes for Cooperstown the first year he was eligible (he needed 336). On the day he won his three hundredth game, he sported a T-shirt that read : 300 WINS IS NOTHING TO SPIT AT.

When Perry announced in his book that he was a "pure, law-abiding citizen" who didn't throw the spitter anymore, manager Gene Mauch responded, "But he doesn't throw it any less, either."

Ed Walsh : The master of the spitter in the days when it was legal, Walsh could make the ball break in, out, up, down, and could even throw it underhand. "It's a puzzle to me," he said of the spitball. "I'll be blamed if I know why it acts that way."

Walsh, an ex–coal miner, won forty games for the White Sox with his spitter in 1908. Interestingly, the only two men to win forty games in a season in this century were spitballers—Ed Walsh and Jack Chesbro. Walsh made it to the Hall of Fame in 1946.

A story is told that Ed Walsh used to wet the ball down by simply sticking out his tongue and *licking* it. After some frustration with trying to hit him, an opposing team came up with a way to fight back—they smeared horse manure on the ball when Walsh came to the mound.

"I vomited all over the place," Walsh recalled.

Eddie Cicotte : Another legal spitballer, he didn't become a big winner until he got a sore arm and turned to trick pitches.

Cicotte would put oil in his glove, rub the seams of the ball in oil and then apply dirt. "The oil would form the perfect base for absorbing the dust," he said.

Ty Cobb said Cicotte threw the most mysterious pitch he'd ever seen. "You could never see it break, but it was almost impossible to get the bat on the pitch," according to Cobb. "He never told his secret to anybody, not even his catcher or manager, and to this day it remains a mystery."

Cicotte won 210 games and left the game the year the spitter was banned. He had to—one of the "Eight Men Out" in the Chicago Black Sox scandal, he threw two of the games himself and was banished from baseball for life.

Lew Burdette: Next to Gaylord Perry, Burdette was the nerviest of the spitballers. When umpires asked to see the ball, he would *roll* it to them, removing any moisture in the process. Burdette's scheme was to spit tobacco juice around the mound area and make little mudpies. When he got to a tight spot, he'd bend down to tie his shoe and wipe a little goo on the ball. Red Smith used to write that newspapers needed three columns for Lew's pitching record—won, lost, and relative humidity.

He was one of the most accused pitchers of the fifties, though he never admitted throwing a spitter. "My best pitch is the one I don't throw," he used to say cryptically. Don Hoak, who hit against Burdette, claimed, "Only once did I ever see water fly off a spitball, and the man who threw me the pitch was Burdette." Somewhere along the line Burdette's spitter got to be a running joke and players used to take the balls he was throwing and write on them, "Spit here, Lew."

Preacher Roe: With a mediocre 34–47 record, Roe was just about washed up before he decided to go illegal in the winter of 1947. He said: "'If I get caught,' I told myself, 'they'll kick me out. If I don't, I'm through anyway, so how can I lose?'" Preacher *didn't* get caught and didn't lose much from that point on. He compiled a 93–37 record for the Dodgers over the rest of his career, including an amazing 22–3 in 1951.

Roe would grab a stick of Beech-Nut gum (his preferred brand) on the bench and say, ''I'm gonna get me a new batch of curveballs.'' His foolproof method on the mound was to spit on the meat of his hand while pretending to wipe his brow. Sometimes to throw off the umpires, Pee Wee Reese or Billy Cox would load the ball up for him.

One of the few to come out of the closet with his spitter, Preacher told the kids of America how to throw a spitter in a 1955 *Sports Illustrated* article. ''If it's a good 'un,'' Roe said of the spitter, ''it drops like a dead duck just when it crosses the plate.''

Burleigh Grimes: ''Ol' Stubblebeard,'' as he was called, was known as one of the meanest men in the game. He walked to the mound with a swagger and peeled back his lips in a yellow-toothed snarl while looking in for the sign. It's been said that Burleigh was so nasty that he once beaned a guy who was standing in the on-deck circle. His baseball career spanned six decades (including coaching, managing, and scouting) and he was elected to the Hall of Fame in 1964.

Grimes won 270 games with his spitball, and his only problem was telegraphing when he was going to throw it. One season hitters were jumping all over his spitter until a teammate figured out why—Burleigh's cap was too tight. Whenever he spit, the action of his jaw muscles moving made the peak of the cap bob slightly. When he was only faking the spitter, he didn't use the jaw muscles and the cap didn't move. Hitters simply watched Burleigh's cap to find out if a spitter was on the way. The solution to the problem—a bigger cap.

During another season, second baseman Pete Kilduff gave away Grimes's spitter. Every time the catcher flashed the sign for a spitball, Kilduff would grab a handful of dirt so that he would be able to get a grip on the ball if it was hit to him. Opponents caught on right away, but it wasn't until years later that somebody told Burleigh everyone knew when a spitter was coming by simply watching Kilduff.

Who Invented the Spitball?

There is one more man who deserves to be in the Spitball Hall of Fame, and he wasn't even a pitcher. George Hildebrand, an outfielder who played just eleven games in the major leagues, invented the spitball in 1902. (Some people give credit to Bobby Mathews, who pitched for Fort Wayne in 1871, but it was certainly Hildebrand who was responsible for spreading the pitch through the major leagues. Besides, his makes a better story, and that's what baseball is all about, isn't it? If Hank Aaron had eaten as many hot dogs as Babe Ruth, he'd be a legend today.)

When the pitching rubber was moved back to sixty feet and six inches in 1893, pitchers began coming up with curves, knucklers, and other baffling pitches to trick batters. Hildebrand came up with the most effective one.

It's not exactly as inspiring as the discovery of penicillin, but Hildebrand stumbled onto the spitter in much the same way that Alexander Fleming made his find. Playing for Providence, a minor league team in the Eastern League, Hildebrand was warming up with a rookie pitcher named Frank Corridon.

"He threw his slow ball by wetting the tips of his fingers," Hildebrand recalled years later. "Just as a joke, I took the ball and put a big daub of spit on it and threw it up to Joe Brown, who was catching. The ball took such a peculiar shoot that all three of us couldn't help notice."

Hildegrand showed Corridon how he did it and Corridon used the new trick in a real game, striking out nine batters in five innings. But he hurt his arm and refused to throw the pitch again.

That probably would have been the end of the spitter, but later that season Hildebrand moved to Sacramento in the Pacific Coast League. There he met a pitcher named Elmer Stricklett, who was about ready to retire from baseball. Hildebrand taught him the spitball and Stricklett won eleven straight games. Stricklett made it all the way to the Chicago White Sox in 1904, where he roomed with a rookie pitcher named Ed Walsh. The success of Walsh and the other legal spitballers led to even more devious trick pitches that involved tampering with the ball.

Ironically, the man who invented the most notorious illegal pitch in baseball history went on to become an American League umpire. George Hildebrand quit playing ball in 1913 and stayed on the other side of the law *watching* for spitballs until 1934—the same year the last legal spitball was thrown. He passed away in 1960, in Woodland Hills, California.

Why Was the Spitball Banned?

While the plain vanilla curve ball was banned the instant it was developed and legalized later, the spitball enjoyed sixteen happy years of legality before it was outlawed. It never dominated baseball, but became a handy out pitch for sticky situations.

Almost immediately, though, some people began to complain that the spitball should be banned. They used a number of arguments, none of which really holds up when examined carefully.

• The most common argument was that the spitball was unsanitary. Baseball was forever trying to create the image of a clean sport that would attract a class crowd, and a bunch of guys gobbing all over the balls did not further that goal.

"There is nothing very pleasant in the sight of a big fellow emptying the contents of his face upon a ball," wrote *Sporting Life* correspondent Ren Mulford, Jr., in 1908. "There's something creepy and 'slimy' in the very suggestion of the spit ball. Perhaps if it were called the 'salivated shoot,' the moist delivery would have better credentials for discussion in good society.''

Mulford, I feel compelled to add, also referred to the spitball as ''a slobber-coated sphere.''

While it's true that throwing a spitball isn't exactly hygienic, no effort has ever been made to prevent hitters from spitting on their hands to get a grip on the bat or fielders from spitting in their gloves. Today, of course, we can't turn on a ballgame for five minutes without seeing players spitting and grabbing themselves in super slo-mo. And don't catch yourself walking barefoot in a major league dugout.

· It was also argued that the spitball was dangerous to hitters, because it is a difficult pitch to control. The same could be said of the knuckleball, of course, and there has been no talk of banning that elusive pitch. In truth, the spitter usually breaks down, out of harm's way. There is no evidence that spitball artists were wilder than any other pitchers. In fact, the year Ed Walsh won forty games, he walked just .85 batter per game.

Burleigh Grimes threw dangerous pitches that hit batters' heads regularly, but that was on *purpose*—with his fastball. He claimed that in nineteen seasons he only hit one batter with his spitball—Mel Ott. Grimes liked to tell the story of the time he was protecting a small lead in the ninth inning with the bases loaded. He intentionally threw three balls to get the hitter looking for a walk, and then struck him out on spitters. That's how good his control was.

· Another argument against the spitter was that it would damage promising young pitching arms. ''It hurts a pitcher in the forearm,'' claimed Cy Young. ''On account of the ball slipping from the moistened fingers with no spinning motion it has to be thrown with a hard snap of the forearm. That is a continuous strain on the muscles just below the bend in the elbow on the inside of the arm. Once those muscles get out of shape, a pitcher is practically gone, so far as a good curveball is concerned.''

Actually, the wrist snap required to throw a *curveball* is probably much harder on the arm than a spitball is. The fact that so many pitchers threw spitters well into their forties shows how *easy* on the arm the pitch must be. Hall of Famer Red "Urban" Faber didn't start throwing a spitter until he got a sore arm, and then used it until he retired at forty-five. Jack Quinn threw his spitter in the big leagues for twenty-three years, and he didn't call it quits until he was forty-nine.

There have also been complaints that the spitball slowed down the game, and that it made it difficult for fielders to handle the ball, but the biggest reason the pitch was banned is far simpler—banning it gave the game more hitting. Babe Ruth had just finished the season with a then-incredible twenty-nine home runs, and fans flocked to ballparks around the country to see the big guy try to sock one over the wall. World War I had just ended. Fans in the Roaring Twenties wanted to see offense, and banning trick pitches would produce it.

Also, rumors were already flying about the fixing of the 1919 World Series. The men who ran baseball were of the mindset to do anything they could to clean up the game's image.

But even the theory that banning the spitter would automatically increase hitting doesn't stand up. Like the knuckleball, the spitball is a very difficult pitch to master. Only one out of ten pitchers in the major leagues threw it regularly even when it was legal.

And the spitball is not unhittable. "It's far easier to hit than legend suggests," says Earl Weaver. In 1965, Milwaukee manager Bobby Bragan ordered his pitchers to throw seventy-five to eighty spitters in a game against the Giants, in an effort to prove that umpires were doing nothing to stop the illegal pitch. Bragan proved his point, but his four pitchers were rocked for thirteen hits, including home runs by Willie Mays and Willie McCovey in a 9–2 rout. The spitball is not a miracle pitch, and a spitter with too much spin on it is a batting-practice fastball.

Should It Be Legalized Again?

If making the spitball illegal doesn't necessarily increase hitting, hurt young arms, put hitters in danger, or make the game more disgusting, why isn't it legalized once again? It's not for lack of trying. Efforts were made to "decriminalize" the spitter in 1949, 1955, 1961,* and 1966. "If I had my way, I'd legalize the old spitter," said none other than former baseball commissioner Ford Frick. "It was a great pitch and one of the easiest to throw."

American League president Joe Cronin was also in favor of legalization, as was Casey Stengel and famous umpires Jocko Conlan and Billy Evans. In more recent years, Sparky Anderson, Frank Robinson, and Tim McCarver have come out in favor of legalization. Frank Frisch, who played both before and after the pitch was banned, said, "The solution is simple—permit the pitchers to wet the ball and get on with the game."

The legalization question is somewhat similar to the controversy over whether or not some illegal drugs should be legalized. We can't stop the flow of drugs into the country, so let's make them legal, regulate them, and stop wasting taxpayers' money trying to stop them, some people say. Similarly, we can't enforce the spitball ban no matter how hard we try, so let's make it legal and stop worrying about it.

On the other hand, if you legalize the spitball, or if you legalize drugs, you're only adding another vice to a vice-rich world. Anti-spitter and anti-drug activists claim that the failure to enforce a law is not a reason to abandon it. As former National League president Warren Giles put it, "We don't catch all the murderers, but we don't legalize murder because of that."

Certainly the way the rule stands now is ridiculous. Pitchers

---

* On November 26, 1961, the Playing Rules Committee voted 8–1 to reject a proposal to legalize the spitball. Oddly, the one vote in favor of legalization came from former umpire Cal Hubbard—the only umpire to eject a pitcher for throwing a spitball in fifty years.

are not allowed to put their fingers in their mouths while they are standing on the mound, but if they simply step *off* the mound for a moment they can do anything they like. That's supposed to prevent spitballs?

Legalizing the spitter could have a positive effect on the game. If the designated hitter in the American League serves mainly to keep aging superstar hitters in the game a few more seasons, legalizing the spitter might do the same thing for pitchers.

Obviously, everyone isn't in favor of legalizing the spitter or it would have been done long ago. The most convincing argument against legalization is the simplest one—the spitball just ain't natural. Roger Craig, father of the split-finger fastball, explained in an interview why the spitball *isn't* fair while his favorite pitch is.

"The spitter is not a *natural* pitch: you're using a gimmick to strike people out. I don't like to see guys scuff the ball or throw spitters, and with the split-finger, you're using your own natural talent to throw."

While it's true that saliva is about as un-foreign a substance as you can get, the fact that a man has to apply *anything* to the ball to make it break is an indication that he couldn't make it do that on his own. Pitchers with overpowering fastballs or wicked natural curves have rarely resorted to spitters, and spitball pitchers have almost never had good curveballs. The spitball, it could be argued, is a crutch for men without natural ability—or men who no longer *have* their ability—to compete against those who do. As Ty Cobb once put it, "Tampering with the ball isn't baseball anyway."

Then there are those of us who are against legalizing the spitball, but for another reason. If the spitball were legal again, it would take all the fun out of it. As long as it's an outlaw pitch, it leads to devilishly clever attempts at deception, wonderful controversy, rumors, accusations, and great baseball stories. Pitchers will keep throwing it whether it's legal or not, so we might as well enjoy the benefits of forbidden fruit.

OTHER WAYS TO SAY "SPITBALL"

Beech-Nut Curve
Country Sinker
Cuban Forkball
Dew Drop
Goo Ball
Greasy Kid Pitch
Gunkball
Money Pitch
Right-Turn Slider

Staten Island Sinker
Sticky Sinker
Super Sinker
The Hair Tonic Terror
The Old Meatball
The Thing
Wet Curve
Wet One

• • • The Unknown Spitballer • • •

What happened to the pitchers who had been throwing the spitball when it was banned in 1920? Unlike silent movie actors when talkies took over, spitball pitchers were *not* forced to change with the times. Each of the sixteen major league teams were allowed to designate two spitball pitchers, who were instructed to continue throwing the pitch for the remainder of their careers.

This "grandfather clause" was applied to eighteen players: in the American League, Doc Ayers, Ray Caldwell, Stan Coveleski, Urban Faber, Dutch Leonard, Jack Quinn, Allan Russell, Urban Shocker, and Allen Sothoron. In the National League, Bill Doak, Phil Douglas, Dana Fillingim, Ray Fisher, Marv Goodwin, Burleigh Grimes, Clarence Mitchell, and Dick Rudolph. Three of them—Grimes, Faber, and Coveleski—made it to Cooperstown.

The unluckiest spitballer was a man named Frank Shellenback, who pitched briefly for the Chicago White Sox in 1918 and 1919. Shellenback happened to be in the minors when the spitter was banned, and the Sox neglected to list his name as a designated spitball pitcher for the 1920 season. Consequently, he was never alowed to pitch in the majors again.

Shellenback went to the Pacific Coast League, where the spitball was still legal, and won an amazing 295 games over fourteen years. Had Chicago simply added him to the list of spitballers, Shellenback probably would have had a productive major league career and might have been in the Hall of Fame today.

• • • Gunkballs in Hollywood • • •

In *It Happens Every Spring* (Twentieth Century–Fox, 1949), Ray Milland plays chemistry professor Vernon Simpson, who is in his laboratory trying to develop a liquid that will keep bugs off trees. Suddenly, a baseball crashes through the lab window, destroys everything and rolls right into the soupy mess.

Surprise! Vernon discovers that the ball now effectively repels wood, which, coincidentally, is what baseball bats are made of. He abandons his sleepy college town and devoted girl (Jean Peters) to become a pitcher with the St. Louis Cardinals.

The kid is a sensation. He hides the gunk in his glove and rubs the ball into it between pitches. Any time a batter swings, the ball does ridiculously loopy dipsy doodles to get around it. In one scene, his catcher has a wooden splint on his hand, causing the ball to roll away whenever he tries to pick it up. In another, his teammates mistakenly use Vernon's gunk as hair tonic, and then comically try to comb their hair with wooden combs.

Simpson wins thirty-eight games and leads the otherwise pitching-pathetic Cards all the way to the World Series. (It's unclear why the folks back home don't make the connection between their missing professor and the hottest new arm in the National League, but that's the movies.) On the last play of the season, Vernon foolishly tries to catch a line drive with his bare hands, ending his pitching career. But all is not lost. He goes back to his girl and is made head of the research department. Catch it on late-night TV sometime.

· · ·

◊ **THEY SAID IT** ◊

• • • • • • • • • • • • • • • • • •

"The anti-spitball rule was designed to prevent 'freak' deliveries. It was punitive and unjust. It was bad for baseball. It still is."

—*Jim Brosnan*

"Spit is a foreign substance."

—*Duke Snider*

"If the spitter is too vulgar for some people, they have no place in baseball or even watching it. Who's to talk about vulgarity anyway, with the stuff you see on TV or in the papers?"

—*Burleigh Grimes*

"It's easy to catch pitchers throwing spitballs. A guy with no sinkerball suddenly develops a great one. You can tell when it drops that the pitch is loaded."

—*Charlie Dressen*

"Every pitcher needs an insurance policy."

—*Mike Flanagan*

"[Bill] Singer had a spitball that could croon 'God Save the Queen' in forty different languages."

—*Bill Lee*

"I used alum, had it in my mouth. Sometimes it would pucker your mouth some, get gummy."

—*Stanley "the Greased Pole" Coveleski*

• • •

◇ THEY SAID IT ◇

· · · · · · · · · · · · · · · · · · · ·

"A spitball is not a dangerous pitch, and not harmful to the arm. It's quite possible some pitchers could add three, four or even five years to their careers if allowed to use the spitball."
            —*Former American League president Joe Cronin*

"There's no use complaining about the spitter, because the umpires are helpless to do anything about it."

                                    —*Gene Mauch*

"Everyone knows that 90% of the pitchers in our league have thrown a spitter at one time or another."
                                    —*Gil Hodges*

"The rule is clear, but it is unenforceable, because how can you prove that a guy threw it? As far as I'm concerned, there aren't any pitchers throwing spitballs, because it's against the rules."
    —*Cal Hubbard,
        supervisor of American League umpires, 1967*

"I like to sit in this easy chair by the window here. That way I can look out at the birds and animals that come right up on the back lawn. . . . I sit here and look out at it all, and I think to myself that everything I've got I owe to the spitball."
                —*Burleigh Grimes, at age seventy-three*

· · ·

◇ THEY SAID IT ◇

· · · · · · · · · · · · · · · ·

"Let them revive the spitter and help the pitchers make a living."

—*Casey Stengel*

"He says You will have to learn to cover up your spitter. He says I could stand a mile away and tell when you was going to throw it. He says Some of these days I will learn you how to cover it up. I guess Al I know how to cover it up all right without Walsh learning me."

—*Ring Lardner, in* You Know Me, Al

"When I broke into the big leagues it was a rare game that used up three baseballs. The home team furnished the umpire with three new baseballs when the game started. If these three were lost or cut beyond all possible use, the local nine would roll out another ball on demand. And they could roll out anything they chose. So strange things happened once the local club got one run in front."

—*Bill Klem, Hall of Fame umpire*

"It would go around the field once or twice and come back to the pitcher as black as the ace of spades. . . . Believe me, that dark ball was hard to see coming out of the shadows of the stands."

—*Fred Snodgrass*

· · ·

◊ THEY SAID IT ◊

• • • • • • • • • • • • • • • • • •

"I once called the president of Vaseline and told him he should use me in a commercial since I use his product all the time."

—*Gaylord Perry*

"One of the few things about baseball that hasn't changed since the turn of the century is the fact that pitchers cheat."

—*Former umpire Ron Luciano*

"I don't put any foreign substances on the baseball. Everything I use is from the good old U.S.A."

—*Relief pitcher George Frazier*

"If you can cheat, I wouldn't wait one pitch longer."

—*Oriole pitching coach George Bamberger, to Ross Grimsley*

"He's a sinkerball pitcher, and like all things that sink, they tend to get wet once in a while."

—*Ron Luciano, about Steve Rogers*

"The spitball is the biggest piece of fiction there is. . . . All a batter has to do is have the umpire look at the ball, because to be an effective spitter, the ball has to be loaded up good."

—*Ted Williams*

• • •

◊ THEY SAID IT ◊

. . . .

"I didn't slop all over the ball. I just nipped a little off a slippery elm tablet on the bench before each inning."

—*Ed Walsh*

"I think that ball disintegrated on the way to the plate and the catcher put it back together again. I swear, when it went past the plate it was just the spit went by."

—*Sam Crawford, about Ed Walsh's spitball*

"When I have fingers run through my hair, I usually get kissed."

—*Don Drysdale, on pitcher searches*

"My mother told me never to put my dirty fingers in my mouth."

—*Don Drysdale*

"He talks very well for a guy who's had two fingers in his mouth all his life."

—*Gene Mauch, about Don Drysdale*

"There has been frequent talk of abolishing it altogether. Of late, however, these rumors have largely died down, and there can be no doubt that the spitball has come to stay."

—Baseball *magazine, 1913*

. . .

◇ **THEY SAID IT** ◇

. . . .

"Mike Garcia threw one at me one time, and the spit came up and hit me in the eye."
— *Ted Williams*

"Hell, if K-Y jelly went off the market, the whole California Angels' pitching staff would be out of baseball."
— *Bill Lee, 1973*

"I have been very fortunate in my life. I've had numerous wonderful experiences. But searching a sweaty pitcher on a humid night is none of them."
— *Ron Luciano*

"What's he throwing," the Whammer howled, "spitters?"
"In a pig's poop." Sam thrust the ball at him. "It's drier than your grandaddy's scalp."
— *Bernard Malamud*, The Natural

Umpire Ed Sudol: Any of your pitchers spit on the ball, captain?
Willie Mays: No sir. We have a team rule that nobody breaks. None of the pitchers ever spit on the ball.
Sudol: Now, you're sure of that?
Mays: Oh sure, the pitcher spits in the glove and then puts the ball there.

• • •

◇ **THEY SAID IT** ◇

· · · · · · · · · · · · · · · · ·

"Hit it on the dry side."
— *Stan Musial, on how to handle spitballs*

"If the spitter comes back, Judas priest, it will turn the game of baseball upside down!"
— *Branch Rickey*

"I often wonder what today's batters would have done against the old trick pitching—like the spitball and the other freaks."
— *Ty Cobb*

"I never threw the spitter—well, maybe once or twice when I needed to get a guy out really bad."
— *Whitey Ford*

"I always thought the rule makers ought to end the hypocrisy and legalize the spitball."
— *Frank Robinson*

"I probably should have cheated more. I should have thrown a spitter."
— *Jim Bouton*

"You put *snot* on the ball?!"
— *Charlie Sheen, in the movie* Major League

· · ·

3rd INNING

The Scuffball

"The bottom line, big brother, is those four umpires accused a Niekro of cheating. They've put a black mark on the Niekro name, which is a shame and an insult to hard-working, God-fearing people like Mom and Dad. Momma raised no cheaters."
—Joe Niekro, in a letter to his brother Phil, 1987

One of the most memorable baseball images of recent years is Minnesota Twins pitcher Joe Niekro with both hands up in the air in the classic "Don't shoot, I give up" pose while surrounded by grim-faced umpires. The scene took place in the fourth inning of a game against the California Angels on August 3, 1987.

After a particularly wicked "knuckleball" to Brian Downing, umpire Dave Palermo marched out to the mound to have a look at Niekro's glove. Finding it clean, he asked Niekro to empty his pockets (a request pitchers may refuse). Niekro flipped them inside out, bringing his hands up in the air. As he did, a five-inch emery board and a small piece of sandpaper contoured in the shape of a finger fluttered to the ground.

Busted in front of 33,938 witnesses!

The umpires immediately ejected Niekro and sent six roughed-up baseballs they had collected from him to Bobby Brown, president of the American League. ("Those balls weren't roughed up," California manager Gene Mauch said later. "Those balls were borderline mutilated.")

Niekro, forty-two years old and nearing the end of his career, claimed that it was necessary to file his nails carefully with an emery board in order to throw a good knuckleball. He had been doing it for sixteen years. He needed to carry the sandpaper, he explained, in case the emery board got soggy.

"They can carry a chain saw as long as they don't use it on the ball," said umpire Dave Palermo. "The guy was so blatant," added the quotable Palermo, "it was like a guy walking down the street carrying a bottle of booze during Prohibition."

Niekro did the usual time (ten days) and the incident touched off a wave of cheating and accusations in the summer of 1987 that harked back to the days of the Wild West.

The First Scuffball

The exclamation "He tore the cover off the ball!" used to refer to power hitters. More often these days, it refers to aging pitchers.

Rule number 3.02 states that "No player shall intentionally discolor or damage the ball by rubbing it with soil, rosin, paraffin, licorice, sandpaper, emery paper, or other foreign substance." Nobody has been caught tossing licorice balls in recent years, but inventive mound doctors have used everything from belt buckles to wedding rings and can openers.

The scuffball has bumped the classic spitter off the sports pages in recent years. It's much easier to throw and control. It can be thrown hard like a fastball, so it's more difficult to hit. A scuffball pitcher doesn't have to mess with gooey substances, figure out ways to hide them, or worry about teammates being reluctant to shake hands with him. And unlike the spitball, he doesn't have to "reload" a scuff on every pitch.

Though it has been popularized recently, the scuffball goes all the way back to 1910. Russ Ford, a twenty-seven-year-old rookie with the New York Highlanders, was warming up under a grandstand in Atlanta one momentous day when one of his pitches got away and banged into a cement post. The next pitch he threw took a very peculiar break. Ford examined the ball and saw a rough spot that had been caused when the ball hit the cement. He began to experiment, cutting the ball with a bottle cap until he learned to control the new pitch.

On April 21, 1910, he used it in a game for the first time. "Never in my life," said umpire Billy Evans, "had I seen a ball do the acrobatic stunts Ford had it perform that afternoon." Russ Ford became the sensation of the American League that year with a 26–6 record.

How to Throw the Perfect Scuffer

A scuffed ball behaves something like the old flat-sided wiffle balls we all had when we were kids. The way to throw a dynamite scuffer ("Kids, we're professionals—don't try this in the Little League") is first to rough up the ball on one of the four round areas that are free of stitching. It doesn't take much.

You want to grip the ball on the seams in such a way that the scuff mark faces either first or third base. You don't want it on the top or bottom. The idea is for the scuff mark to stay in one place as the ball rotates, so it will disrupt the airflow on that one side. The ball will break toward the side opposite the scuff. If you want the ball to break to the left, grip it so the scuff is facing third base (to your right). If you want the ball to break to the right, put the scuff facing first (to your left). Throw the ball just like you would throw an ordinary fastball, with backspin. See how it spins around the scuff so the rough part stays in one place? You're on your way to becoming a major league cheater.

The hard part isn't throwing the scuffball—it's getting the scuff on the ball without anyone noticing. Russ Ford had a neat trick. He fastened a piece of emery paper to a string and hitched the other end of the string to the inside left sleeve of his undershirt. His glove had a hole cut in the center of it (as was the custom in those days) so he could pull the emery paper through the hole and scuff up the ball.

It was also the custom for fielders to toss their gloves in foul territory at the end of the inning. Ford would simply pull the emery paper back through the glove, into his sleeve, and drop the glove, keeping the emery on him.

Everyone has their own style. Some pitchers use a belt buckle or one of the sharp eyelets on their glove, or even a plain old sharp fingernail. Ferguson Jenkins filled the seams of the ball with dirt, and Dave Danford used paraffin. If the umpire isn't too attentive, you can one-hop your last warm-up pitch into the dirt deliberately. It will produce a natural scuff mark and you can start the inning with a beat-up ball.

Razor blades work even better. During his umpiring days, spitball inventor George Hildebrand once picked up a new baseball and noticed that one of the stitches had been neatly sliced with a razor blade. Hildebrand thought it might be a good idea to check the others in the box, and discovered that every one had been cut in the exact same way. Allen Sothoron of the St. Louis Browns brought a razor right out to the mound with him. He'd cut slits into the cover of the ball and raise the surface slightly with his finger. When he left the mound at the end of the inning, he'd smooth the slit marks down again.

Clark Griffith didn't bother with any extra hardware at all. He simply banged the ball against his spikes, pretending to knock the mud off them. That's the same Clark Griffith, by the way, who was one of the most vocal about banning the spitball when he was president of the Washington Senators.

The *inside* of the ball has not been neglected by mound doctors. "To loosen the cover on a ball, the pitcher grasps the ball with both hands and twists in opposite directions," wrote *The Literary Digest* in 1923. "A pitcher with powerful hands is able to do this. We have seen it done."* Baseballs are made better now, but pitchers have been known to insert phonograph needles into the balls and poke BB shot under the horsehide. The rumor about Hall of Famer Ted Lyons was that he got his pitches to fly erratically by stuffing the balls with Mexican jumping beans.

It helps for a pitcher to have teammates who are handy with hardware. Catcher Birdie Tebbetts attached thumbtacks to his shin guards, which not only served to cut the ball nicely, but

---

* There was once a minor league player named Billy Scripture who was so strong that he could break a bat by grabbing its barrel with one hand, the handle with his other, and twisting in opposite directions. Scripture was also known to stand in front of pitching machines and let the balls bounce off his chest, to bite the covers off balls, and to take bites out of the bench. (I've heard of riding the bench, but *eating* it?) It's unfortunate that such a colorful eccentric never made it to the majors.

also must have made those close plays at the plate all the more exciting.† Billy Meyer was even more obvious—he hung a vegetable grater on the back of his glove. Why the umps didn't spot that is a mystery for the ages.

Leo Durocher used to scuff the ball for Dizzy Dean, and Elston Howard did the job for Whitey Ford. Norm Cash's second favorite trick (after corking his bat) was to toss the clean game ball into the dugout at the beginning of an inning and give pitcher Hank Aguirre the battered infield practice ball. What are teammates for?

The Scuffball Hall of Fame

While the Spitball Hall of Fame was mostly old-timers, the Scuffball Hall is composed of recent players, some of them still active. The spitball was *the* illegal pitch of the past; the scuffball is the illegal pitch of today.

It doesn't take much to make a name for yourself as a scuffballer. Between them, Phil and Joe Niekro won more than five hundred baseball games and had long and brilliant careers. But when you say "Niekro," one thing comes to mind for most baseball fans—emery boards. It's unfortunate that an embarrassing five-minute incident would taint forty years in the big leagues, but that's baseball.

These, then, are the nominees for the Scuffball Hall of Fame . . .

Whitey Ford: No relation to Russ Ford, the multitalented Whitey threw a spitter, mudball, *and* a scuffer, riding them to 236 victories and a plaque in Cooperstown.

---

† Tebbets was an illegal pitcher's best friend. On one occasion he was catching spitballer Tommy Bridges with Joe Gordon of the Yankees at the plate. After a loopy spitter, Gordon dove at Tebbets, trying to get the ball and show it to the umpire. Birdie's quick response was to heave the evidence into left field, where it dried off before the next pitch.

Ford went to the trick pitches when it mattered most. In 1956, he made a two-hundred-dollar bet with Giants owner Horace Stoneham that he could get Willie Mays out in that year's All-Star game. Ford won the bet because, he says, "I threw Willie the biggest spitball you ever saw." He also admits to having loaded a few mudballs in the World Series. He would make little mud pies in the grass behind the pitcher's mound and load up while tieing a shoelace. In a 1963 Series game against the Dodgers, Whitey says, "I used enough mud that day to build a dam."

Whitey told all in a 1977 book and a *New York Times* article titled "Confessions of a Gunkball Artist." His gunk—or "magic elixir," as he called it—was a homemade concoction of turpentine, baby oil, and rosin that he kept hidden in a roll-on deodorant bottle. "I'd put it on both hands, on my uniform shirt, on as many places as I could," Ford admitted.

Ford was never nabbed, but one time his gunkball got Yogi Berra in trouble. It seems that Yogi was a mooch. Instead of buying his own toiletries, Yogi was constantly using everyone else's. Knowing this, Mickey Mantle put Ford's deodorant bottle in a spot where Yogi was sure to see it. Sure enough, Yogi took the bait and used the stuff on himself.

"The next thing we heard was Yogi hollering and bellowing things like, 'Son of a ——, what the hell is this stuff?' " says Ford. Berra's arms were literally stuck to his sides. The Yankee trainer used alcohol to dissolve the stuff, but in the end they had to shave Yogi's armpits.

Whitey's tour de force was his scuffball. He paid a jeweler friend a hundred dollars to build a ring with a half-inch-by-quarter-inch stainless-steel rasp. He'd wear the ring on his right hand—his glove hand—and wrap a flesh-colored Band-Aid around the ring to hide it. In pressure situations, Whitey would simply take off his glove, step off the mound, and rub up the ball with his ring. He'd flap his glove to indicate to catcher Elston Howard which way the freak pitch was going to break.

"Whenever I needed a ground ball, I'd cut it good," he

recalled. "It was as though I had my own tool bench out there with me."

Ford's scuffing career came to an end in Cleveland one day. Opposing pitcher Jim "Mudcat" Grant (he of soapball fame) picked up a ball Ford had used the previous inning, noticed the gouge marks and showed it to the umpires. Rather than push his luck, Ford got rid of his ring and never used it again.

(Jim Bouton tells the story slightly differently. He says the umpire went out to the mound and said, "Whitey, go into the clubhouse. Your jock strap needs fixing. And when you come back, it better be without that ring.")

At least in Whitey's day, when you got caught cheating, the whole world didn't see it on the evening news that night.*

Mike Scott: After learning to throw the split-finger fastball, Scott became one of the most dominating pitchers of the last five years. And one of the most whispered about.

"The question on everyone's mind is, 'Does Scott doctor the ball?'" says Tim McCarver. "The answer is yes, of course." The problem has been catching him. There is some circumstantial evidence: Leon Durham of the Cubs found a piece of sandpaper behind the mound at Wrigley Field during one of Scott's games, and opposing teams have collected dozens of baseballs with half-dollar-sized scuff marks in the same place on each one. But umpire Doug Harvey checked Scott sixty-five times during the 1986 season and found nothing.

How Scott is getting away with it is a mystery. The consensus is that no man goes from a seven-year career high of 137 strikeouts to an astonishing 307 the next season without a little extra help.

Don Sutton: Over his long and productive career, Sutton acquired such a reputation as a scuffball artist that his nick-

---

*It's also worth noting that Whitey once made a commercial in which he debated Salvador Dalí on the issue of whether a knuckleball or a screwball is easier to throw.

name became ''Black & Decker.'' Telephoto lenses have been trained on him, videotapes analyzed, and umpires have virtually undressed him on the mound, but nobody has ever caught Sutton in the act and he has never admitted any wrongdoing.

''Somehow a mysteriously scuffed ball got into the game,'' Sutton once told reporters with a straight face. ''I don't like them in the game. It would be too hard to throw them straight.''

In 1978, Doug Harvey ejected him from a game for scuffing balls. Sutton actually threatened to sue Harvey if he was going to be suspended, on the grounds that it would be depriving him of earning a living. The league backed off and said Don wasn't ejected for doctoring baseballs—he was ejected for *throwing* baseballs that happened to be doctored. Baseball is a game of subtle distinctions.

Still, Sutton knew he had a good thing going and kept his sense of humor about the whole business. On one occasion, an umpire went out to the mound to check Sutton's glove for sharp objects and discovered a note inside that said, '' YOU'RE GETTING WARM, BUT IT'S NOT HERE!''

Tommy John: A medical miracle who had a tendon from his right wrist implanted into his left elbow, John was best known for his slice. According to Earl Weaver, TJ's signature was three sharply cut lines with a scuff mark in the middle.

Taking all the accusations in stride, when the umpires searched him on the mound, he liked to tell them, ''Look out, you're going to cut your finger on that razor blade.'' He has never been caught.

When asked how many pitches he had, John once responded, ''Four basic ones—fastball, curve, slider, and change-up, plus eight illegal ones.'' When he pitched for the Yankees, he kept a statue of Jesus above his locker, which may or may not have some significance.

◇ YOU COULD LOOK IT UP ◇
• • • • • • • • • • • • • • • • •

"The pitcher's glove may not be white or gray."

"A QUICK RETURN pitch is one made with obvious intent to catch a batter off balance. It is an illegal pitch."

"No player shall intentionally discolor or damage the ball by rubbing it with soil, rosin, paraffin, licorice, sand-paper, emery-paper or other foreign substance."

"When the bases are unoccupied, the pitcher shall deliver the ball to the batter within 20 seconds after he receives the ball."

"Neither the pitcher nor any other player shall dust the ball with the rosin bag; neither shall the pitcher nor any other player be permitted to apply rosin from the bag to his glove or dust any part of his uniform with the rosin bag."

• • •

Jim Bunning: The fact that Bunning is now a United States Congressman in Kentucky's 4th District makes his selection to the Scuffball Hall of Fame all the more special. In his playing days on the Detroit Tigers, Bunning was a notorious "buckle-baller." Teammate Hank Aguirre says he once found a grinding machine in a back room behind the Tigers' clubhouse, and he and Bunning used it to file Bunning's belt buckle until it was razor sharp. "You could slice your finger off on his belt buckle," claimed manager Gene Mauch.

Now that ballplayers wear double-knit uniforms without belts, scuffballers have to use other tools to do their dirty work. Fortunately, Bunning is in politics, where there is no need for dishonesty.

In 1987, Jim Bunning missed being inducted to Cooperstown by just four votes.

Rick Rhoden: "I think he scuffs the ball with sandpaper," says Philadelphia Phillies centerfielder Lenny Dykstra. "We all do." During a game in 1986, New York Mets first-base coach Bill Robinson crossed paths with Rhoden at the end of an inning and told his ex-teammate, "You're too good a pitcher to cheat." One thing led to another, and both benches cleared in one of the more memorable baseball brawls of the season.

Rhoden has pitched (and been accused of cheating) in both leagues. Umpires have collected balls he has thrown in which a scuff mark has been rubbed right over the words "American League." But in a game against Texas in 1988, he was more aggressive. Umpire Larry Barnett told *The Village Voice* that one of the balls he collected from Rhoden looked like it had been worked over with a chisel, and opposing manager Jim Snyder said, "One of the balls we managed to get looked like it had an open cab door hanging off the side of it."

Rhoden, like most of the suspected scuffballers, has never been caught.

The Most Blatant Scuffballer

Catching scuffballers *should* be easy. The only real advantage the spitter has over the scuffer is that you can quickly wipe the ball down to dry it off when the umpires start closing in. Once a ball is scuffed, it *stays* scuffed. That being the case, it's remarkable that more scuffball artists are not caught.

Besides the hall of famers above, the "usual suspects" in scuffballing have been Hank Aguirre, Tom Bergmeir, Tom Estell, Kevin Gross, Ferguson Jenkins, Dennis Leonard, Ted Lyons, Mike Marshall, Ray Miller, Jim Perry, Nolan Ryan, Dave Smith, Tim Stoddard, and Early Wynn. Of these, only Gross has been caught with his hand on the cookie cutter.

Ray Miller, who became a pitching coach after his career was over, keeps a collection of balls thrown by renowned scuffballers. The prize possession of this museum of scuff art is a 1978 Dennis Leonard that Miller claims he retrieved before it ever touched the ground.

That's pretty much all anybody can do—collect balls. After Nolan Ryan beat them 1–0 in 1988, the Dodgers collected three dozen balls that were scuffed in the same spot. When Mike Scott pitched a one-hitter against them in 1987, they sent the league office a dozen balls Scott had allegedly scuffed. After a game against the Yankees a few years ago, Indians manager Pat Corrales held up a deeply cut ball and told reporters, "Boys, there's Tommy John's sinker. And we've got more balls just like it."

That and a dollar, as they say, will get him on the subway. It doesn't matter how many battered baseballs are lovingly collected and sent to baseball officials. It's not enough evidence to convict. It may make umpires watch a guy more carefully, but collecting baseballs is otherwise a waste of time. Balls are often scuffed when they hit the dirt, wall, or backstop. They might have been scuffed intentionally by an opposing team that's out to get a particular pitcher. To be punished for throwing a scuffer, a pitcher practically has to be caught on the mound with an ax in his hand.

That's virtually what happened to Rick Honeycutt, in the most blatant scuff incident in baseball history. While Niekro and others could argue that emery boards and sandpaper are necessary tools for precision nail filing, there wasn't much Honeycutt (with the emphasis on the "cutt") could say in 1980 when caught on the mound with a *thumbtack* sticking through a Band-Aid on his finger.

Catching Honeycutt "was about as difficult as spotting a whale in a bathtub," according to umpire Nestor Chylak. He became the first pitcher to be ejected for throwing a scuffball since they were banned exactly fifty years earlier.

Umpire Bill Kunkel (he who threw a spitter in his playing days) was behind the plate, and even before the game had started he was asked by the Kansas City Royals to check Honeycutt. By the third inning, Kunkel had collected three balls, each with three slashes across them. After an unnaturally great curveball to George Brett, he went out to the mound and grabbed Honeycutt's hand.

"Son," Kunkel said, admiring the hardware, "take a hike."

Hal McRae, the next batter, spotted a piece of sandpaper near the mound. Handing it to the umpires, he said, "Here, you might as well have the whole kit."

Even more embarrassing for Honeycutt, when he went to wipe his brow, he forgot about the thumbtack and walked off the field with a bloody scratch mark across his forehead.

Later, in the safety of the clubhouse, Honeycutt was boasting, "I thought the thumbtack trick up all by myself. Pretty smart, huh?"

Honeycutt was nabbed in the last weekend of the season, so his suspension had to carry over all the way to the next year. Despite the humiliation, Honeycutt resumed his career successfully and pitched, for the World Champion Oakland Athletics, in the 1989 World Series.

Other Leagues

Long after trick pitches were banned in major league baseball, they were still perfectly legal in the Negro leagues. "Lefty" Sam Streeter was the acknowledged master of the spitball, while

Smokey Joe Williams was known for using a gooey, black substance as well as sandpaper. With a limited budget, the Negro league umpires rarely tossed a ball out, so as the games progressed the baseballs got grimier and grimier.

One memorable day in 1930 came to be called "the Battle of Butchered Balls" in the black press. Williams, pitching for the Homestead Grays, went up against Chet Brewer of the Kansas City Monarchs and they held nothing back. In twelve innings of spit, mud, scuffs, tar, and who knows what else, the hapless hitters were only able to push one run across the plate. Brewer struck out nineteen batters and Williams, in an afternoon that never made the record books, fanned an unbelievable twenty-seven.

"The rules were broken very flagrantly in some of the exhibition games I used to play against the Negro leagues," recalls Bob Feller. "They got away with murder. But they weren't fooling anyone. I told one of them one time, 'Either knock it off or you're not making any more stops with us.'"

According to Feller, Satchel Paige never tampered with the ball, though he did occasionally pitch half a foot in front of the rubber (a trick Rudy May perfected years later).

The top Negro league teams also made it a point not to play so hard that they would overwhelm their opponents with too many runs. "When they were out on the road, they were ordered sometimes not to win by too much," says Donn Rogosin, author of *Invisible Men: Life in Baseball's Negro Leagues*. "They wanted to put on a good show so they could come back and play a rematch."

But for real baseball corruption, spend a season in the Mexican, Dominican, or Cuban leagues, where the Negro league stars often went in the off-season. When Dominican political strongman Rafael Trujillo decided he wanted his team to win the Dominican pennant, he didn't fool around. Future Hall of Famer Cool Papa Bell and his teammates lost a game one day, and they were greeted at their hotel by militiamen who shot rifles in the air and shouted, "El Presidente doesn't lose!'' Needless to say, the team swept their next series.

Bill Lee played winter ball in Cuba one year, and he says that on one occasion Castro's soldiers trained their rifles on a baserunner at third and said he would be shot if he tried to score.

Perhaps the most unusual baseball is being played in Japan, where they love the game but have altered it slightly to suit the national temperament. American players have gone over there and been bewildered to find that games have a time limit of three hours and twenty minutes, and teams are happy to play for a tie score.

To avoid embarrassing players, umpires make calls in such a way as to even things out. If a player (especially an American player) has been hitting a lot of home runs, the umpire will expand his strike zone to give the other fellows a chance.

But at the same time, the Japanese don't want to perform poorly, and take the responsibility of losing very seriously. In 1988, general manager Shingo Furuya of the Hanshin Tigers was so despondent about the problems of his last-place team that he leaped out of his hotel to his death.

Other Tricky Pitches

There is nothing in the official baseball rules that specifically prohibits the ''kimono ball,'' yet it has only been thrown once in major league history—and that was in a spring training game.

This wacky pitch was invented by left-hander Tommy Byrne of the Yankees in 1955, mostly to amuse fans on a tour of Japan. He would go into his regular windup, but instead of releasing the ball he would continue his arm around and fling the ball at the plate in a high arc from behind his back. The batter was usually too shocked to move, much less take a swing.

The eccentric Casey Stengel couldn't help but be charmed by the kimono ball and gave Byrne the go-ahead to use it in a game. On March 26, 1956, he tossed it to a dumbfounded Pee Wee Reese. We will never know if it was a ball or a strike, because umpire Larry Napp ruled it a "discard" and warned Byrne to knock off the funny stuff. According to *The Crooked Pitch,* Martin Quigley's epic on the curveball, the kimono ball is the only pitch declared illegal in this century because of its delivery.

Another wacky trick pitch is the blooper (the lob, the balloon, dewdrop, eephus, folly floater, LaLob), which has had an occasional moment in the sun over the years. The pitcher simply lofts a ridiculously high, lazy lob at the plate and overanxious hitters can't help but take exaggerated cartoon swings. Rip Sewel had some success and notoriety with it in the forties and Steve Hamilton kicked up some controversy throwing it in the seventies. After some debate, the American League ruled that the pitch was legal, but the National League banned it.

However, a check with Bill Deane, senior researcher at the National Baseball Hall of Fame, shows that as long as a pitcher doesn't put a foreign substance on the ball or violate the balk rules, there is nothing in the official rules that puts a restriction on his delivery. According to Deane, when a pitch has been declared illegal, it has been a judgment call by the umpire. If the umpire feels a guy is throwing silly pitches and making a mockery of the game, he will rule it illegal.

There *is* something in the rules about beanballs, which *are* illegal. "To pitch at a batter's head is unsportsmanlike and highly dangerous," read the official rules. "It should be—and is—condemned by everybody. Umpires should act without hesitation in enforcement of this rule."

Well, it's not condemned by *everybody*. Managers commonly order their pitchers to throw beanballs, especially after one has been thrown at a teammate. In 1939, after Ducky Medwick and Pee Wee Reese were beaned out of the lineup, the Dodgers complained about "Beanball, Incorporated"—a supposed conspiracy to knock off the team one by one and kill their pennant chances. Burton Turkus, who led the real Murder, Inc., investigation, was even called in to solve the case.

A baseball—in most cases, anyway—is harder than a head

and the knockdown pitch has been an effective way for pitchers to keep hitters from getting too comfortable. ''For all its art,'' says Roger Kahn, ''major league pitching is largely a business of terror.''

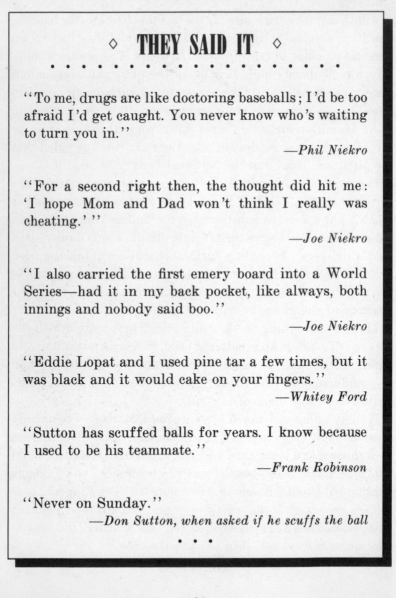

⬦ **THEY SAID IT** ⬦

• •

''To me, drugs are like doctoring baseballs; I'd be too afraid I'd get caught. You never know who's waiting to turn you in.''

—Phil Niekro

''For a second right then, the thought did hit me: 'I hope Mom and Dad won't think I really was cheating.' ''

—Joe Niekro

''I also carried the first emery board into a World Series—had it in my back pocket, like always, both innings and nobody said boo.''

—Joe Niekro

''Eddie Lopat and I used pine tar a few times, but it was black and it would cake on your fingers.''

—Whitey Ford

''Sutton has scuffed balls for years. I know because I used to be his teammate.''

—Frank Robinson

''Never on Sunday.''

—Don Sutton, when asked if he scuffs the ball

• • •

The man who didn't start it all : Abner Doubleday.
(*National Baseball Library, Cooperstown, N.Y.*)

The 1894 Baltimore Orioles. The dirtiest—and perhaps the smartest—team in baseball. (*National Baseball Library, Cooperstown, N.Y.*)

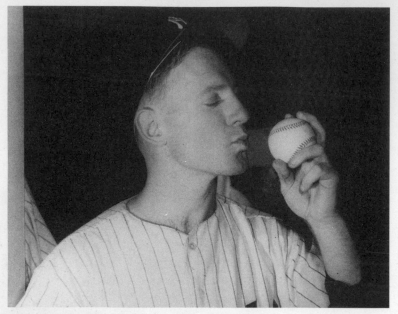

They didn't call him "Slick" for nothing. Whitey Ford was a master of what he called his "gunk ball." Today, he's a Hall of Famer. (*National Baseball Library, Cooperstown, N.Y.*)

Some guys just can't take a joke. The first baseball commissioner, Kenesaw Mountain Landis, was brought in to make baseball wholesome again after the Black Sox Scandal in 1920. (*National Baseball Library, Cooperstown, N.Y.*)

Ed Walsh. The spitball was legal in his day, so he just stuck out his tongue and licked the ball. In an inspired moment, his opponents rubbed horse manure on the ball before tossing it to Ed. (*National Baseball Library, Cooperstown, N.Y.*)

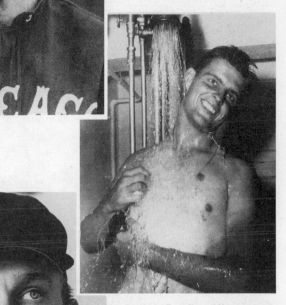

A young Don Drysdale prepares to throw his wet one. (*National Baseball Library, Cooperstown, N.Y.*)

Isn't baseball ironic? Umpire Bill Kunkel admitted that when he was a pitcher, he threw a pretty good spitter. (*National Baseball Library, Cooperstown, N.Y.*)

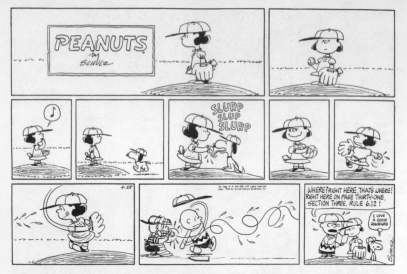

Actually, it's Rule 8.02. (*Copyright © 1963 by United Features Syndicate, Inc. Reprinted by Permission.*)

Yes, baseball certainly is ironic. Former outfielder George Hildebrand, who has been credited as the inventor of the spitball, went on to become a longtime American League umpire. (*National Baseball Library, Cooperstown, N.Y.*)

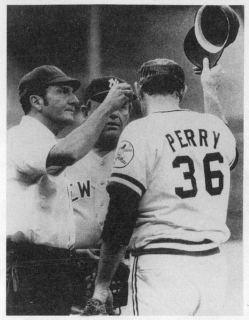

The most notorious spitballer ever, Gaylord Perry
got used to being strip-searched on the mound. Here,
umpire Lou DiMuro admires Perry's hairdo in
1973. Despite the fact that he had the nerve to entitle
his autobiography *Me and the Spitter*, Perry was
caught only once in his twenty-year-plus career.
(*National Baseball Library, Cooperstown, N.Y.*)

Joe Niekro caught red-handed. He parlayed the incident into an appearance on
"Late Night with David Letterman." (*Associated Press/Wide World Photos*)

Wearing his "Coke bottle" glasses, Ryne Duren would intentionally toss his last warm-up pitch over everyone's head to make hitters think he was wild. Son, Steve, and wife, Beverly, look like they'd be pretty tough on the mound, too. (*National Baseball Library, Cooperstown, N.Y.*)

Russell Ford, inventor of the scuffball. (*National Baseball Library, Cooperstown, N.Y.*)

Eddie Stanky leaving Ford Frick's office in 1950 after being told to stop performing "the Stanky Maneuver"— jumping up and down and waving his arms crazily at second base to distract batters at the plate. (*National Baseball Library, Cooperstown, N.Y.*)

Former Tiger Norm Cash demonstrates the form that he used in his playing days. (Sports Illustrated)

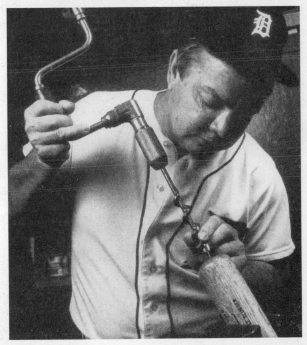

Some people believe The Babe tampered with his bats. (*National Baseball Library, Cooperstown, N.Y.*)

Corking and Other Forms of Bat Mutilation

"I owe my success to expansion pitching, a short right field fence and my hollow bats."

—Norm Cash

Consider for a moment how tough it is to hit a baseball. You're standing at home plate facing a major league power pitcher. He stands sixty feet and six inches away, but because of his height he releases the ball fifty-five feet from you. His fastball moves between 90 and 100 miles per hour (Nolan Ryan was once clocked at 100.9, and Ty Stofflet, a softball pitcher, at 104.7). The average 90 MPH fastball reaches you 41/100ths of a second after it leaves the pitcher's hand (50/100ths at 80 MPH). In order to hit the ball, you've got to make your decision to swing after seeing just 13/100ths of a second of its trajectory. "If you swing for distance," says Mickey Mantle, "you almost have to have the bat in motion before the pitch is even released."

It gets tougher. Baseball is unusual among sports in that the hitting instrument is smaller than its target. You're trying to hit the ball with a thin round bat, which is considerably more difficult than hitting with a flat object, as in tennis or golf. With a round bat and a round ball, the difference between smacking a line drive and missing entirely is 12.1 centimeters up or down the barrel of the bat.

Then there's the timing of your swing. A difference of one millisecond will make a hit go over second base or down the foul line. If you swing a mere three milliseconds too early or too late, you miss the ball entirely. Baseball may be a game of inches, but hitting is a game of milliseconds and millimeters. And as Stanford physicist Paul Kirkpatrick says, there are twenty-six ways to fail in every attempt to hit a baseball.

It gets tougher still. Even if you can whack somebody's fastball, the pitcher may very well cross you up with a curveball, sinker, change-up, forkball, split-finger fastball, knuckleball, or some illegal pitch he's got up his sleeve. He may throw the ball inside, outside, high, low, or straight at your head. To hit a home run, which is what most batters today seem to be swinging for, you've got to slam that ball with 1,400 pounds of force.

It gets even harder. The whole time you're attempting to pull off this remarkable feat, millions of people are watching your every twitch on TV, thousands in the stands are screaming that you're a bum, and a few are calling for the pitcher to stick it in your ear.

You're damn straight, hitters cheat.

Ted Williams said that hitting a baseball is the single most difficult thing to do in sport, and there hasn't been much argument in forty years. A .300 hitter, we are often reminded, fails 70 percent of the time. Where else in life can a person fail 70 percent of the time and be considered outstanding? With numbers like that in any other business, they'd throw you out on the street. In baseball, you're a hero.

Despite the fact that rules are constantly being tweaked to help the hitters—making the ball more lively, banning trick pitches, moving the fences in, lowering the mound, and shrinking the strike zone—hitters are constantly struggling to keep up with the pitchers. To get any edge they can, many batters resort to tactics that do an end-run around the rule book.

How to Cork a Bat

"I batted .283 for Andy Cohen in '54, and he took me with him to Double-A New Orleans the following year," recalls Earl Weaver. "That was when I was introduced to the incalculable benefits of using a corked bat."

Bat corking is by far the most popular way for hitters to cheat. According to the rules, a legal bat must be a solid piece of wood. (One odd exception—it is legal to use a bat made of several pieces of wood glued together, though I have yet to hear of anyone using a "plywood bat.") Earl Weaver never made it to the majors as a player, but he *did* hit six home runs one month in the minors with his corked bat before the league president was tipped off that every bat on the team was loaded. "The umpires raided our clubhouse like they were the Untouchables," he says. "They destroyed the bats in public, right on the field. I wanted to cry." Weaver didn't hit another homer that season.

How do you do it? Simple. Bore a hole about one inch in diameter and a foot deep into the meat end of the bat, being careful to line up the drill and the bat perfectly so the wood doesn't split. Clean out the wood shavings and pack the hole with cork, sawdust, Styrofoam, or any other substance that is lighter than wood. Then plug the mouth of the hole with plastic wood that matches the color of the rest of the bat. Sand the top of the bat smooth. Rub on a dollop of pine tar to make it look used. *Voilà!* Superbat. It takes about a half an hour. If you've done a good job, nobody will be able to detect any tampering, even with a magnifying glass.

Do corked bats really work? It's debatable. Ballplayers almost unanimously agree that a ball hit in the air off a corked bat travels as much as fifty feet farther than one hit with a legal bat. Scientists who somehow manage to convince their universities that they should be studying such matters aren't so sure. Whether they work or not, as you read this some guy is probably swinging a bogus bat in the big leagues. The estimates are that from 5 to 30 percent of all hitters tamper with their bats in some way.

Sometimes they get caught. In 1981, Dan Ford of the California Angels was ejected from a game for using a corked bat. In 1987, the Astros' leading hitter Billy Hatcher had his bat split open as he was beating out an infield hit against the Cubs. Third baseman Keith Moreland showed the umpires the bat and Hatcher was ejected from the game. He claimed that his regular bats were broken and that he had borrowed the illegal bat from relief pitcher Dave Smith, but that didn't wash with the commissioner's office. Hatcher was suspended for ten days.

The best bat-loading incident took place in 1974, when Graig Nettles took a bat-breaking cut and sent six Super Balls raining across the infield of Yankee Stadium. Catfish Hunter later revealed that it was reserve catcher and accomplished woodworker Ed Hermann who had loaded Nettles's bats for him.

Like pitchers, some hitters wait until their careers are over before spilling the beans. Norm Cash of the Tigers was a notorious corker, and even posed for a photo layout in *Sports Illustrated* demonstrating how he had doctored his bats during his playing days.

"Any one of Norm's bats would have given a metal detector a nervous breakdown," jokes former umpire Ron Luciano. (Why a metal detector would detect cork is something only an umpire would understand.)

When Cash came to bat in crucial situations, opponents would yell, "Check his bat!" and he would go back to the dugout and get some legal lumber before the umpires had the chance to check him. He led the American League by hitting .361 in 1961, but it's hard to give all the credit to cork—the next year Cash hit .243.

When he retired in 1984, star outfielder for the Kansas City Royals Amos Otis revealed that he had used a corked bat for the last fourteen years of his career. Otis was never ejected, but he *was* caught once in 1971. His doctored bat split open after hitting a line drive, and home plate umpire Nestor Chylak simply kicked it out of the way so a sliding runner wouldn't get injured. Back in those innocent times, Otis only got a warning for breaking the rules of the game.

"I had enough cork and Super Balls in there to blow away anything," Otis remembered. "Over my whole career, it probably meant about 193 home runs for me." Otis, by the way, had a career home run total of 193.

Aside from the convicted corkers and guys who admitted it later, it's all a matter of speculation. After he was traded in 1980, Dave Rader said a local carpenter kept the Phillies supplied with corked bats. John Mayberry said the same about Kansas City after he was traded to the Blue Jays. Earl Weaver became convinced that Cecil Cooper used a doctored bat when he saw Cooper hit a home run against the Orioles one-handed.

When the Twins were accused of corking by the California Angels in 1984, Minnesota manager Billy Gardner replied that "they could use [California third baseman] Doug DeCinces's bats for fishing bobbers." This points out one reason why the players only rarely accuse their opponents of cheating—often they're cheating themselves and don't want to call unnecessary attention to it.

Howard Johnson is probably most often accused among current players. Johnson, who had hit twelve, eleven, and ten home runs in 1984–1986, suddenly walloped thirty-six for the Mets in 1987. Suspicions arose, especially after *New York Newsday* reported that someone in Houston had sent one of Johnson's bats to the offices of the National League, where it was found to be corked. Because the bat wasn't confiscated through normal channels, no punishment was doled out, but umpires and opposing managers began watching Johnson carefully and X-raying his bats regularly ("He ain't Babe Ruth," claimed Whitey Herzog).

Johnson was never officially caught using a corked bat, but the Elias Sports Bureau conducted a statistical study showing that after opposing managers started checking his bats on August 6, Johnson's home-run production dropped from 3.44 to 2.45 per 100 at-bats. This fluctuation, according to Elias, would occur by chance only once in 3,309 trials. The suggestion is that Hojo had been corking, but stopped when they started X-raying his bats. In 1988, he dropped down to twenty-four home runs and allegations weren't as frequent. In 1989, he had hit twenty-two by the All-Star break, and opposing managers started checking his bats again.

Unless they're caught red-handed, we never know for sure who's cheating and who isn't. But here is a list of hitters who have been suspected of bat tampering.

NAMING NAMES:
HITTERS ACCUSED OF BAT DOCTORING

Tony Armas	George Foster	Candy Maldanado
Jose Cardenal	Bobby Grich	Buck Martinez
Norm Cash	Ken Griffey	Graig Nettles
Vince Coleman	Toby Harrah	Ben Oglivie
Cecil Cooper	Hawk Harrelson	Darrell Porter
Vic Correll	Bob Horner	Dave Rader
Doug DeCinces	Howard Johnson	Mike Schmidt
Rick Dempsey	Ted Kluszewski	Ken Singleton
Len Dykstra	Davey Lopes	Duke Snider
Dan Ford	Hal McRae	Andre Thornton

Other Ways Hitters Cheat

Batters don't have nearly as many options for skullduggery as pitchers do, but corking a bat is by no means the only thing they can do to cheat. Anyone who has watched a baseball game has seen the first hitter up meticulously erase the rear white line of the batter's box with his shoe. Rod Carew was famous for this. By standing a few inches farther away from the pitcher, he had a few more milliseconds to look over a pitch before deciding whether or not to swing. Most fans don't even call that cheating.

The hitter's only weapon is his bat, and if he can do something to make the ball travel farther, more power to him. In the fifties, Ted Kluszewski of the Cincinnati Reds was known to sink ten-penny nails into his bat barrel to make it harder. George Sisler would bang brads into his bats. When umpires discovered this, Sisler purchased blue Victrola needles from a music store, rammed them into the bat and honed them down with a ham-bone.

Anything you can do to enlarge the hitting surface on a bat should increase the chances of making contact. Baseball experimented with flattened bats back in 1885, but they were banned after one year. Bob Feller claims that in his day, guys would peel away one side of the bat's wood to make a homemade flat surface. Nellie Fox, among others, achieved the same result by slamming his bats with a sledgehammer. Bobby Bonds once recalled that when he was a rookie he spent four hours smoothing down one side of his bat to make better contact.

"In my first at-bat it broke," he recalled. "I never doctored a bat again."

During a game in 1982, umpire Bill Kunkel took a close look at Toby Harrah's bat and saw that the handle had been sawed off and refastened with glue and a wooden peg. The bat was confiscated, but no further action was taken against the Cleveland slugger. Harrah claimed he hadn't sawed up his bat to generate more power; he only wanted to shorten it because his shipment of new bats hadn't arrived.

The fact that he was hitting .400 at the time made it all the more suspicious. It's fine to use a trick bat if you hit .190, but if you're threatening baseball's immortals, you'd better be doing it fair and square.

As hitters depend on their bats to earn a living, it stands to reason that they would treat them with tender loving care. Players used to spend countless hours rubbing their bats with soupbones and soda bottles to harden them, though "boning your bat" is somewhat of a lost art today.

The range of legal (but weird) things hitters do to their bats is unlimited. Joe DiMaggio, an Italian all the way, used to rub olive oil into his bats. Honus Wagner boiled his in creosote. Eddie Collins, it was said, buried his bats in a dunghill during the off-season. If you don't think hitting is a labor of love, consider that "Shoeless Joe" Jackson was known to take his bat "Black Betsy" to bed with him.

Both Babe Ruth and Ted Williams considered their bats so important that they traveled down to the Hillerich & Bradsby factory in Louisville, Kentucky, to personally pick out the

◇ YOU COULD LOOK IT UP ◇

· · · · · · · · · · · · · · · · · ·

"The bat shall be a smooth, rounded stick not more than 2¾ inches in diameter at the thickest part and not more than 42 inches in length."

"The bat shall be
(1) one piece of solid wood, or
(2) formed from a block of wood consisting of two or more pieces of wood bonded together with an adhesive in such a way that the grain direction of all pieces is essentially parallel to the length of the bat."

"No laminated bat shall be used in a professional game until the manufacturer has secured approval from the Rules Committee of his design and method of manufacture."

"A design or method of manufacture which produces a 'loaded' or 'freak' type of bat or which produces a substantially greater reaction or distance factor than one-piece solid bats will not be approved."

"The bat handle, for not more than 18 inches from its end, may be covered or treated with any material or substance to improve the grip."

· · ·

◇ YOU COULD LOOK IT UP ◇

• • • • • • • • • • • • • • • • • • •

"A batter is out for illegal action when he uses or attempts to use a bat that, in the umpire's judgement, has been altered or tampered with in such a way to improve the distance factor or cause an unusual re-action on the baseball. This includes bats that are filled, flat-surfaced, nailed, hollowed, grooved or covered with a substance such as paraffin, wax, etc."

• • •

---

lumber. Williams would search for narrow-grained wood, while Ruth preferred a piece of wood with knots in it.

The dark grain of wood is softer than the light grain. Former Yankee shortstop Tony Kubek, now an announcer, admits that he and his teammates (who included Roger Maris and Mickey Mantle) used to carve out the soft, dark grain on their bats with an icepick. Then they would smear pine tar into the grooves, let it harden, and sand it down to give their bats a harder surface. The words "pine tar," of course, immediately bring to mind a little incident involving George Brett and an illegal bat, but we'll get to that later.

As long as you're carving grooves into your bat, why fill them up? Horizontal grooves cut into the barrel of the bat serve to put backspin on the ball upon impact, similar to the scoring on the face of a golf club. The backspin makes the ball hang in the air longer and travel farther than one that isn't spinning. In 1975, both Bill Buckner and Ted Simmons were caught with carefully grooved bats. Buckner had just driven in a run with his and Simmons had a home run taken away. Both men were called out.

Hitters will go to ingenious lengths to tamper with their bats.

In 1982, *Sport* magazine reported an anonymous Chicago hitter inserted three metal rods down one side of a bat to make that side heavier. When the batter swung the bat rods-down, it would drive the ball up and increase his chances of hitting a fly ball. With the bat rods-up, a grounder could be purposely hit. The bat was never popular, possibly because it couldn't do the one thing hitters want to do when they step to the plate—hit a line drive.

Graig Nettles tells of a teammate in the minors who went to even more elaborate lengths to doctor his bat. Instead of loading it with cork or metal rods, he inserted a tube of mercury into the heart of his bat. When the bat was held upright, it would feel very light. But when he swung it, the centrifugal force would cause the mercury to rush up the barrel, moving the center of gravity and making the bat swing like a bludgeon.

Brilliant! Unfortunately, this genius was never very skilled at putting his miracle bat on the ball and he never made it to the majors.

Did the Babe Cheat?

Even the immortal Babe Ruth, years after his death, has been accused of tampering with his bats. It was well known that the Babe carved a notch into the trademark of his bat for every home run hit with it, and at Hillerich & Bradsby, home of the Louisville Slugger, there is a Ruth bat with twenty-one notches in it. But in 1983 Ruth was posthumously accused of doing more with cork than popping it out of champagne bottles.

The Seattle Mariners were in Baltimore for a game, and the clubhouse man was showing some of the players a 36-ounce, brown Louisville Slugger with Ruth's signature on it. Supposedly, the Bambino had given the bat to a cousin of his in 1929. The Seattle players were admiring this piece of history reverentially when outfielder Dave Henderson noticed that the round end of the bat didn't exactly match the wood of the barrel. The end was cracked, but the rest of the bat was not.

"That's a plug!" said Henderson. "This bat is corked!"

The suspect bat was never X-rayed. "I never heard anything about it at all while I was doing research," says Ruth biographer Bob Creamer. Unless the National Baseball Hall of Fame and other repositories of Ruth bats decide to investigate the lumber, we'll never know for sure whether or not the Babe—every American boy's baseball hero of the century—was a cheater.

Bat Chat

Actually, it's doubtful that Babe Ruth would have intentionally corked his bats. Not that Ruth was any angel—far from it. But in his day it was commonly believed that the heavier the bat, the faster and farther a man could hit a ball. Now, in the "lite" era, we know it's the exact opposite. Today's players cheat to make their bats lighter, which is the purpose cork serves. If Ruth cheated, he would have most likely done something to make his bat *heavier*, like driving in nails as Kluszewski and Sisler did. In fact, old-time players used to refer to a bat as a "piece of iron."

In his prime, Ruth hoisted a 42-ounce club to the plate, and that wasn't even the heaviest. Edd Roush, who played for the Giants and Reds, is credited with using the heaviest bat ever— 48 ounces. (The lightest bat was used by Solly Hemus—29 ounces.) Ruth once ordered a 50-ounce bat, but only used it for practice. As he got older he ordered progressively lighter bats, and was using a 35-ouncer at the end of his career.

Though Ruth used heavy bats, he actually contributed to the trend of bats getting lighter. The players in his day wanted to swing from the heels like the Babe did, but most men could barely lift those 40-ounce clubs. In those days, bat handles were quite thick, nearly as thick as the barrel. Rogers Hornsby was one of the first to use a tapered bat, with more weight at the barrel. Heinie Groh of the New York Giants took this to ridiculous extremes with his weirdly shaped "bottle bat."

In recent decades, bats have come to resemble exclamation points. The great hitters like Ted Williams, Rod Carew, and Stan Musial used light bats, in the range of 31–33 ounces. Roger Maris whacked his sixty-one home runs with a 33-ounce bat. Hank Aaron was known for using one of the lightest bats in the game, and he hit more home runs than anybody. Some experts believe bats have gotten lighter as a result of fastballs getting faster. It's simply too hard to get a 40-ounce club around fast enough to hit a 90 MPH heater.

According to Hillerich & Bradsby, 36-ounce bats were the norm before 1950. In the next decade it dropped to 34–35 ounces, and today bats that weigh 31–32 ounces are in the greatest demand. They used to make them out of hickory (as in "the old hickory") and Harmon Killebrew once experimented with a bat made of maple, but almost all bats are now made of forty- to fifty-year-old prime white-ash trees grown in upper New York State and Pennsylvania. Baseball bats are one of the few things that truly *do* grow on trees—about sixty can be carved out of each one.

The problem with the trend toward lighter bats is that wood isn't the strongest substance in the world. Drilling a hole into a bat to cork it weakens the wood, as does legally thinning the handle to make it lighter. Bats seem to shatter more and more these days, and some baseball people claim that the wood is inferior to old-time bats. More likely, as thinner, lighter bats have become fashionable, they have simply proved weaker than the old fat bats. Jim Rice, it is said, once swung a bat so hard that it broke—even though he missed the ball completely.

What can be done about corked, grooved, nailed, and otherwise doctored bats? In their infinite wisdom, baseball officials have decided to allow managers to confiscate one bat from the opposing team during each game. Interestingly, this ruling has added a new wrinkle to baseball strategy: when to check the bat.

New York Mets manager Davey Johnson likes to ask for a bat to be confiscated in the early innings, so the hitter won't be able to use it for the rest of the game. Whitey Herzog of the Cardinals takes the opposite approach. If you use up your bat confiscation at the beginning of the game, reasons The White Rat, "everyone on the bench can go get their corked bats because the umps can't check anymore."

The obvious solution to the doctored-bat problem, of course, would be to stick an X-ray machine—like those at airports— in every major league on-deck circle. Of course, the challenge would then simply be to devise a doctoring technique even the X-ray couldn't reveal.

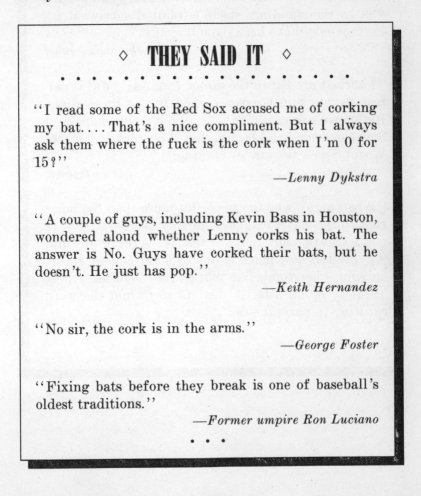

◇ THEY SAID IT ◇

• • • • • • • • • • • • • • • • • • •

"I read some of the Red Sox accused me of corking my bat.... That's a nice compliment. But I always ask them where the fuck is the cork when I'm 0 for 15?"

—*Lenny Dykstra*

"A couple of guys, including Kevin Bass in Houston, wondered aloud whether Lenny corks his bat. The answer is No. Guys have corked their bats, but he doesn't. He just has pop."

—*Keith Hernandez*

"No sir, the cork is in the arms."

—*George Foster*

"Fixing bats before they break is one of baseball's oldest traditions."

—*Former umpire Ron Luciano*

• • •

◇ **THEY SAID IT** ◇

. . . .

"I say if they challenge a bat and it is corked, then suspend the player for life."
—*St. Louis Cardinals manager Whitey Herzog*

"I think it's got to be stopped because every record that's set, every home run that's hit, every game that's won in the standings itself is tainted somewhat because it may have been done illegally."
—*George Steinbrenner*

"I corked my bat in the minor leagues . . . did it perfect too. . . . But I never corked in the big leagues. Fuck, you can get in trouble. What would happen if they suspended ya? Damn, that'd be weak to miss the World Series because of corking."
—*Lenny Dykstra*

"When a guy who has never hit more than ten home runs in the major leagues suddenly hits forty, you've got to question how much of that is the result of working out and how much is due to other causes. In my opinion, when totals like that go into the books, there ought to be an asterisk next to them and the word *cheating* in parentheses."
—*Ozzie Smith*

. . .

Other Ways of Getting an Edge

"That's not cheating. Just a little gamesmanship."
—Manager Maury Wills, after being suspended for having the batter's boxes in the Seattle Kingdome drawn a foot too long.

The Refrigerator Ball

A baseball isn't a complicated object and there are only so many things you can do to it. You can spit on it or scuff it, as we have seen, but those are crude manipulations. There's a more insidious tampering that is easier, more effective, and harder to detect—freeze it.

When the temperature of a baseball goes down, the cork and rubber inside lose their elasticity. The ball doesn't compress and rebound off the bat like a room-temperature baseball. The "coefficient of restitution" (a fancy way to say "bounciness") drops, and home runs become easy fly balls. A night in the freezer does the trick.

If a "refrigerator ball" is removed a few hours before game time, the surface will warm up while the core of the baseball will still be frozen. So it feels like a regular baseball. It's a great equalizer; if your team can't hit with power, neither can anybody else.

Many clubs have tried the old frozen-ball trick, but the good-pitch, no-hit Chicago White Sox of the mid-sixties were masters. According to catcher Jerry McNertney, it was Eddie "the Brat" Stanky, who managed the team in 1966–1968, who did the dirty work, especially when hard-hitting teams like the Yankees came to town.

"You had to wipe the mildew off the balls before the game," McNertney revealed in Jim Bouton's *Ball Four*. "First you'd take them out of the boxes, which were all rotted away anyway, wipe the mildew off and put them in new boxes. Then you'd give them to the umpires and they never suspected a thing."

Opposing players knew all about it. "When our power hitters made contact, it was like hitting a rock and the ball didn't go anywhere," says Jim Kaat, who pitched for Minnesota in those days. Tiger pitcher Hank Aguirre said he could tell the balls had been tampered with in the first inning. "I thought something was funny when the first two batters hit the ball and it went 'Splat!'"

If a light-hitting team can stick the balls into freezers, a power team can just as easily stick them in an oven to make them jump off bats. The Tigers and White Sox got into a cheating match of sorts in July of 1965. One weekend in Detroit, the two teams played a four-game series in which an astonishing eighteen home runs were hit (eleven by Detroit). The next weekend they played a *five*-game series in Chicago and not a single home run was hit. The White Sox claimed the Tigers heated the balls, and the Tigers claimed the Sox froze them. Most likely, they were both right.

This chapter will cover some of the ingenious (and not so ingenious) ways men have cheated besides the usual spitting, scuffing, and corking that have been in the sports pages recently. What can be done to a bat, a ball, the diamond, a body, or an opponent's mind to get an edge?

Creative Groundskeeping

Before a game in 1981, Oakland manager Billy Martin noticed something weird about the batter's boxes in the Seattle Kingdome. He had umpire Bill Kunkel measure them and it was discovered they had been drawn a foot too long in the direction of the pitcher.

The groundskeeper was called on the carpet, so to speak, and admitted the nasty truth—Seattle manager Maury Wills had instructed him to make the boxes too long. Wills (who once authored a book titled *How to Steal a Pennant*) said he was "shocked and dumbfounded" at the accusation that he was playing tricks so his hitters could get to curveballs before they broke. Guilty or not, he was fined and suspended for two games.

Home-field advantage means more than just having the crowd on your side. Diamond doctoring is one of baseball's great traditions. On the surface, whatever you do to a field affects both teams equally and should be deemed fair. But that assumes all teams are created equal. If the home club has a tremendous bunter, for example, it would be to their advantage for borderline bunts to roll fair. If they've got slow-footed fielders, they would want batted balls to roll as slowly as possible. A few years ago, Wade Boggs claimed that home plate in Tiger Stadium was crooked, presumably so Detroit right-handers could more easily work the outside corner.

Subtle manipulations of the playing field can neutralize a team's advantage or disadvantage. Some diamond doctoring is legal (the height of the grass, for example) while some is not (the height of the pitcher's mound).

The most famous diamond doctors were the Bossard family (Emil, Harold, and Marshall) who tended Cleveland Stadium in the fifties. These fellows didn't just come out in the fourth inning and smooth the dirt. During spring training, the Bossards studied the Indians to see how the field could be built for their strengths and weaknesses. Before each game, they would custom-build the field to the team's advantage. If Bob Lemon was pitching, for example, they'd make the infield soft to absorb his grounders. For strikeout artist Bob Feller, they would leave it hard.

The Bossards literally sculpted the field. On his first appearance in Cleveland, Phil Rizzuto beat out three bunts for hits. The Bossards went to work and the next day, every bunt Rizzuto attempted rolled foul.

The fact that Cleveland has only won three pennants since 1903 can hardly be blamed on the Bossards. We can only guess how much worse the team would have been *without* them. When the Indians *did* reach the World Series in 1954, the team voted the groundskeepers a three-fourths share of their winnings.

"I wouldn't be surprised if he helped us win as many as ten games a year," manager Lou Boudreau said of Emil Bossard. Maybe he should have won the MVP that year.

Emil passed away in 1980, but the Bossard family continues their tradition of superior groundskeeping to this day—with the Chicago White Sox.

When sculpting the perfect infield for the home team, the easiest part to carve is the pitcher's mound, which is supposed to be exactly ten inches high. Fastball pitchers love the abnormally high mound in Dodger Stadium, and Shea Stadium in New York is said to be on the lofty side as well. The mound at Wrigley Field, on the other hand, is low. Connie Mack, it's said, built mounds as high as twenty inches, in order to add to the illusion that his fastballers were throwing off a mountain.

It's also common for the home team to slightly alter the visiting team's bullpen mound, so relief pitchers will feel just a bit awkward when they come into the game.

Water can be an excellent tool in the hands of a skilled groundskeeper. A good squirting around first base prevents pesky base stealers from getting a good jump. Water in the power alleys is just what a slow outfielder needs to cut off what would otherwise be an extra base hit. Wetting the infield slows down the ball so your aging third baseman can reach hard-hit grounders. Sinkerballers love it, especially if the dirt around the plate has been softened up a bit.

When Ty Cobb was in his prime, he laid down perfect bunts in the Detroit infield, which was called ''Cobb's Lake.'' Willie Mays says that if they parked cars in the Candlestick Park infield, they'd sink to the hubcaps. Atlanta, San Francisco, Detroit, Boston, and Wrigley Field in Chicago are known swamps. St. Louis, on the other hand, keeps its infield dry and hard so its speedsters aren't slowed down slogging through the mud.

A wet infield was the deciding factor in the 1962 pennant race between the Giants and the Dodgers. Most teams rake their infield, but Giant manager Alvin Dark got word that every morning the Dodgers were *rolling* theirs to create a fast track for Maury Wills (who stole 104 bases that year). With three weeks of the season remaining and the Dodgers coming into town with a small lead, Dark knew he had to stop Wills to stop the Dodgers.

"That morning I ordered our groundskeeper to flood the area around first base," he recalled. "By game time it was a quagmire."

When the umpires asked about the mush, Dark replied, "Gee, I dunno. The sprinklers must have broke or something."

The umps tried pouring dirt around the base, but that only made it softer. It was like running in a sandbox. Wills was furious and didn't steal a single base that night. The Giants swept the series and went to the World Series.

Another trick is to manipulate the height of the grass. Teams with slow fielders almost always grow the grass high. Howard Berk, former vice-president with the Yankees, says that when sinkerball specialist Mel Stottlemyre was on the staff, "we just never cut the grass for several days before he pitched." These days, according to octogenarian pitcher Tommy John, the infield at Tiger Stadium is like the rough at the U.S. Open.

If all else fails, move the fences. Teams routinely build their stadiums to suit the characteristics of their hitters. If you lack power hitting, move the fences farther away so opposing teams' long drives become outs. When Pittsburgh acquired right-handed power hitter Hank Greenberg in 1947, they moved the left-field fence in to catch more of his home runs. That area of the stands came to be called "Greenberg Gardens." Even John McGraw, the last holdout of the home-run era, shortened his right-field line.

If there is one thing that has taken all the fun out of creative groundskeeping, it's artificial turf. There's not much you can do to a field when it's rolled out in one piece. The "carpet" has changed the game so that owners tailor their team to the field instead of the other way around. The St. Louis Cardinals, for instance, are more attracted to young speedsters than home-run hitters in order to take advantage of the fast track.

But even in this age of fake grass, somebody will always come up with a way to manipulate a batted ball to the home team's advantage. When the Cardinals lost the 1987 World Series, Ozzie Smith suspected the answer was blowin' in the wind—air blowers turned on and off strategically in Minnesota. In his book *Wizard,* Ozzie says:

"A couple of the balls we hit in the Metrodome were hit solidly, but once they got to a certain point in the outfield, they seemed to stop. Yet some balls that the Twins hit, once they got to the same point, seemed to carry. I don't have any proof that it was the blowers, and it may or may not be true, but in the back of my mind I will always wonder whether they had something to do with why the Twins were such a different team at home and on the road. Maybe the blowers were on when they were hitting and off when the other team was up."

In fact, Minnesota scored thirty-three runs at home in that Series and just five in St. Louis. Smith wasn't crazy about the Metrodome all around and claims that "whoever built the place should be locked up in an insane asylum."

Illegal Sign Stealing

It's not necessarily illegal to steal signs—it all depends on how you go about it. If you have a guy on second who sees what the catcher is flashing and relays signals to the batter, that's fine. If you have a guy in the centerfield stands with high-power binoculars and a cordless phone connected to the dugout, that's another story.

Since the turn of the century, whatever technology was available has been used for state-of-the-art stealing. In the telegraph age, the 1898 Philadelphia Athletics rigged up a wire that stretched underground from the centerfield clubhouse to the third-base coaching box. Utility catcher Morgan Murphy was stationed in the stands with binoculars, relaying the catcher's signs via Morse code. The third-base coach would receive the signal through a steel plate in the ground and let the batter know what the next pitch was going to be.

The plan worked like a charm until an opposing third-base coach—Tommy Corcoran of Cincinnati—got his spikes caught in the wire and followed it across the field as he yanked it up.

In the radio age, the White Sox installed a transmitter in pitcher Early Wynn's cap so Al Lopez could communicate with him on the mound. And after Bobby Thompson hit his "shot heard round the world" to win the pennant for the Giants in 1951, rumors spread that a buzzer system had tipped Thompson off to the pitch.

In the TV age, Billy Martin is believed to have installed a closed-circuit camera in the Arlington Stadium outfield when he was managing the Texas Rangers. Coach Jim Fregosi, it is said, would watch the game in Martin's office and give the catcher's signs to Martin through a walkie-talkie. (Conversely, in 1986, manager Hal Lanier had all television sets *removed* from the Houston clubhouse because the players spent too much time watching "Wheel of Fortune" when they were supposed to be taking infield practice.)

We can only guess what electronic skullduggery is going on as managers embrace the computer age.

But sign stealing doesn't necessarily rely on technology. (Hell, John McGraw used to indicate steal by spelling out S-T-E-A-L in sign langauge!) At the old Polo Grounds, a guy in the cen-terfield clubhouse would raise and lower a venetian blind to indicate fastball or curve to thankful New York Giant hitters. The Cubs have often been accused of using the same trick in Wrigley Field. In Cleveland, a spy used to relay stolen signs to Indian batters by moving the eyes of a painted Indian on the fence. In Philadelphia in 1910, they turned a weather vane on a house outside the stadium north or south to tip off the next pitch. In Detroit, they simply covered and uncovered a portion of a letter "B" on the wall.

Of course, in these days of highway stadiums and electronic

scoreboards, it's getting harder to pull off devious sign stealing of any sort.

Even TV and radio broadcasters have been known to do their part for the home team. During his days as a color man, Dizzy Dean would communicate to the Cardinals' dugout with hand signals. And Phil Rizzuto, who has worked for the Yankees for nearly fifty years, has attempted to call the dugout from his perch in the press box to let the manager know an opposing runner missed a base for a possible appeal play.

The most unusual sign stealer was probably Bernie Brewer, the team mascot in Milwaukee County Stadium. Bernie, whose main function was to slide down a pole into a giant vat of beer whenever a Brewer hit a home run, was suspected of putting on white gloves to signal fastball and taking them off for curves.

Stealing signs is not a hard science. Even if you have the other team's signals cold, there's no guarantee a hitter will know what's coming. In 1948, Chuck Dressen stole a catcher's sign and told Joe ''Ducky'' Medwick to expect a curve on the next pitch. Ducky leaned in and an inside fastball fractured his skull, ending his career.

Trick Plays

Here's the play: Germany Schaefer of the old Washington Senators is on first and there's a runner on third. Schaefer breaks for second, hoping the catcher's throw will allow his teammate to scamper home. The only problem is, the catcher doesn't throw.

So Germany is on second and his teammate is still at third. On the next pitch, in a burst of inspiration, Schaefer runs back and steals *first*! This gives him the opportunity to try again. That's exactly what he does, and this time the catcher throws. Too late, and the runner on third comes home.

Once an occasional strategic ploy, backward baserunning isn't seen in the game anymore—they passed a rule that banned it, saying that it "made a travesty of the game." You don't poke fun at baseball and get away with it, even if you're just trying to win a ballgame.*

Baseball has nothing so cornball as football's old Statue of Liberty play or so beautiful to watch as a gracefully turned double reverse. But because managers almost always go by the book and "play the percentages," an unexpected trick play is often successful. These are a few of the most popular ones...

The Hidden-Ball Trick: The most famous and humiliating of all trick plays. Gene Michael used to pull it off regularly when he played with the Yankees. Instead of quickly returning a ball to the pitcher, an infielder will hide it in his glove and wait for the runner to take a lead. When he does, the infielder puts the tag on him.

There are variations on the theme. Sometimes a pitcher will throw over to first so many times that the runner *assumes* the ball has been thrown back. Lefty Gomez used to enhance the illusion by putting the rosin bag in his glove with the white showing. John Mayberry, who played first base, wasn't so subtle. He'd simply ask the runner to move his foot so Mayberry could use the base to tie his shoe. The runner stupidly would, and Mayberry would tag him out.

Jimmy Piersall fell for the hidden-ball trick when he played for the St. Louis Browns:

"I hit a double off the wall. After sliding in, I got up and dusted myself off, and then Billy Hunter, their rookie shortstop, asked me to step off the base and kick the bag into line. I looked over at the umpire, Charlie Berry, and I got the feeling it was all right. So I stepped off the base, and Hunter, who

---

* In the fourth inning of a rainy game in 1972, the Tigers and Brewers put on a particularly shameful display. Down by one run and trying to stall so the rain would wash out the game, Tiger outfielders purposely let easy fly balls drop. The Brewers, on the other hand, wanted to get the game over with before the downpour. Their baserunners begged to be tagged out, but the Tiger fielders refused. Both managers were fined for this behavior, despite the fact that no rules were broken and they clearly were trying to win.

had the ball hidden in his glove, tagged me out. That was the most embarrassing play of my life."

Casey Stengel recalled that when he was a boy, he would pull off the hidden-*potato* trick with his brother Grant. Casey, who pitched in those days, would make a pickoff attempt on the runner at second. Instead of returning the ball to Casey, second baseman Grant would toss over a baseball-sized potato he had hidden in his pocket. When the runner stepped off the bag, Grant nailed him with the real ball. Once the Stengel brothers pulled this off in a hostile neighborhood and had to run all the way home.

(Potatoes come in handy in baseball. See "9th Inning" for an even more remarkable spud trick.)

The Precision Play: Casey Stengel attempted another trick play when he managed the Dodgers, but with little success. With a man on third and a right-handed batter up, the pitcher would simultaneously throw at the batter's head and scream, "Watch out!" The batter would dive out of the way—theoretically at least—the runner at third would freeze for a moment, thinking wild pitch. The catcher would then whip the ball to third and trap the runner off base. The only problem was that the third baseman would usually freeze, too, and the pickoff throws went into left field.

Sleeper Rabbit: This one was invented by the old Ty Cobb Tigers, and is one of the few trick plays that can be pulled off by the team at bat. Runners are on second and third. After each pitch, the runner at second intentionally dawdles getting back to the bag. Eventually the catcher will notice this and attempt to pick him off. The moment the ball leaves the catcher's hand, the two runners break for third and home. The team in the field is helpless. In recent years, the Montreal Expos have pulled this one off occasionally.

Cobb and his teammate Sam Crawford had another play that baffled opponents. If Cobb was at third and Crawford could work out a walk, he would jog to first and then suddenly sprint toward second without stopping. The pitcher didn't know if he should go after Crawford or make sure Cobb didn't come home. "Most of the time they were too paralyzed to do anything," said Crawford.

The most igenious trick play I've heard about was cococted by the Florida Technological University team and described by Joe Garagiola in *It's Anybody's Ballgame*. The University of Miami was up with a fast runner on first in a steal situation. As the runner broke, somebody in the Tech dugout whacked two bats together loudly. The catcher caught the pitch and tossed a high pop-up to the shortstop, who yelled, "I got it, I got it!" The runner, having heard the crack of the bat and the shortstop calling for the catch, assumed the batter had popped up. Instead of taking his rightfully stolen base, he hightailed it back to first, where he was out by a mile.

Genius. Pure genius. And perfectly legal.

Annoying Distractions

Pitching effectively and hitting a baseball solidly require an incredible amount of concentration. Anything that can be done to upset that concentration may throw off an opponent's rhythm and provide the edge in a close contest. Now we're getting into baseball psychology, which can be just as potent as any trick play, corked bat, frozen ball, or sculpted infield.

Concentration is a fragile thing. Firpo Marberry's hat would fly off as he delivered the pitch, a calculated diversion. Johnny Allen tore the sleeves of his uniform so they'd flap in the wind. During one game against the Cubs, the home-plate umpire instructed Fernando Valenzuela to go back to the clubhouse and remove some flaps on his shoes. Hitters complained that the flaps interfered with their view of the ball.

But if your mission is to distract a guy, there's no reason to be subtle. You might as well let out a scream at the batter as the ball is approaching the plate, as Casey Stengel did. When George Brett comes sliding into second on an obvious double-play force, he likes to holler at the top of his lungs to rattle the shortstop.

Eddie Stanky was the master of distraction. During a game in 1950, a hitter requested that the second-base umpire move out of his line of vision. Stanky, playing second, thought about that for a moment and promptly filled the same spot. He proceeded to leap and hop about erratically while the pitcher was winding up.

As he perfected this annoying tactic, opponents became progressively more irritated. In a game against the Phillies, catcher Jack Kramer threw his bat all the way to Stanky and both benches emptied. Stanky was thrown out of the game and a new sentence was thrown in the rule book: "No fielder shall take a position in the batter's line of vision, and with deliberate unsportsmanlike intent, act in a manner to distract the batter."

"I was just out there trying to help win a ballgame," claimed Stanky. "If someone pulled that on me, I'd shake his hand—and try to hit past him."

More recently, Wade Boggs got similar treatment from the Minnesota Twins. Just as a pitch was being released, Greg Gagne and Steve Lombardozzi would switch positions at shortstop and second base. It didn't help. Boggs went 9 for 14 in the series, and umpire Joe Brinkman told the two Twins to knock it off or he'd throw them both out of the game.

Catchers have the best opportunity to distract, as they squat right behind the hitter and are usually talkative fellows. Yogi Berra, Bill Dickey, Gabby Hartnett, and Thurman Munson were experts. A frequently used trick is to toss a handful of dirt on the batter's shoes as the pitcher is winding up, or better yet, to spit on them, as Tony Pena has been known to do on occasion.

"I'll do anything so their mind isn't a hundred percent on hitting or the pitch," says Gary Carter, whose favorite ploy is to make the hitter laugh as the ball is approaching.

Ray Fosse liked to butter up the batter, telling him how great he was and how watching the guy play was like poetry in motion. He'd keep it up until the hitter would tell him to shut up, or make physical threats.

A hitter or runner with chutzpah can frequently upset a pitcher's concentration enough to cause a balk. In the thirteenth inning of a tie game in 1974, Diego Segui was about to pitch with runners on first and third when Twins batter Jerry Terrell reached down for a handful of dirt. Segui got rattled and balked in the winning run.

Tito Francona was even more bold. During a game against Boston in 1962, he was on first with the bases loaded and Earl Wilson on the mound. Just as Wilson went into the windup, Francona shouted, "Hold it, Earl! Hold it!" as if time had been called. Instead of going through with the pitch, Wilson stumbled off the mound and balked in the winning run. All's fair in love and baseball.*

Bench Jockeying and Other Humiliations

To truly throw a man off his rhythm, it helps to use a little psychological warfare while distracting him. "A baseball jockey," wrote the *Saturday Evening Post* back in 1941, "is a fellow who yells coarse, crude remarks at the gents of the opposition for the express purpose of covering them with confusion and frustration."

Somewhat of a lost art today, over the years imaginative name calling has ruined good players, made big-mouthed utility men valuable, and even decided the World Series. Umpires take it seriously. During one game in 1946, fourteen members of the

---

* One day while he was third-base coaching the St. Louis Cardinals, Miller Huggins yelled to Dodger rookie pitcher Ed Appleton to let him have a look at the ball. Even though the bases were loaded, Appleton tossed the ball to Huggins, who simply stepped aside and let it roll to the fence. Two runners scored and the Cards won. After the incident, the rules were changed so that coaches are now prohibited from doing anything to draw a throw from the other team.

Chicago White Sox were ejected simply for heckling. When Chicago was in the field, their dugout was empty.

Ballplayers have never been known for their sensitivity. After Tiger manager Hughie Jennings accidentally leaped headfirst into an empty swimming pool one day, opposing teams took delight in screaming, ''How deep was the water?'' at every opportunity. When Frank Robinson was arrested for carrying a concealed weapon in 1960, Lew Burdette of the Braves showed up at the next game wearing a pair of six shooters and holsters over his uniform.

Ted Williams, often criticized by fans and press, once popped off and said, ''Nuts to this baseball. I'd sooner be a fireman.'' Almost immediately, most players in the American League had developed piercing imitations of sirens and other appropriate sound effects to be used whenever Williams came to the plate.

Anything to get a guy mad. If you could make him yell back, you knew you were getting to him. ''It was considered fair game to try to probe for a guy's weak spot,'' said Hank Greenberg, ''so you could catch his attention and destroy his concentration.''

The poor guy with big ears is sure to hear himself referred to as a taxi with both doors open. When the fat guy comes to bat, it's almost inevitable that somebody's going to complain to the umpire that it's illegal for two men to hit at the same time. Particularly ugly guys or guys with funny names are sitting ducks. Charlie Kerfeld (225 pounds) simply looks *too* much like comedian John Candy for anyone to remain silent for long.

Guys like Leo ''Stick It in His Ear!'' Durocher and Billy Martin were particularly vicious. Dick Williams, Toby Harrah, Bobby Valentine, Rick Sutcliffe, and Kurt Bevacqua are skilled jockeys. Often teams have a ''designated bench jockey''—a utility player who is better with the mouth than bat or glove and has little chance of getting in the game and risking retaliation.

The 1939 Cleveland Indians became known for their constant complaining, and when third baseman Ken Keltner applied for unemployment insurance during the off-season, the rest of the league started calling the team the "Cleveland Crybabies." Baby bottles and diapers mysteriously appeared on their dugout walls. Fans sang "Rock-a-Bye, Baby" outside their hotel. Opponents rolled baby carriages out on the field before games.

Bench jockeying has even been the deciding factor of the World Series. In 1940, Schoolboy Rowe appeared on a radio program with his fiancée and happened to ask her, "How'm I doin', Edna?" During the Series, opposing Cincinnati players yelled the phrase so often and so mercilessly that Rowe could barely pitch. He lost two games, gave up twelve hits in 3.2 innings and ended up with an ERA of 17.18.

Bench jockeying still goes on, but these days, players who yell funny things at opponents are considered barbarians. The sensitive men of the 1990s don't want to hurt each other's feelings. Besides, nowadays everybody has the same agent and guys switch teams so frequently that they're often playing against their old buddies. And when you're playing on a team full of millionaires, it's considered undignified to rank on somebody's mother.

• • • Bench Jockeying the Babe • • •

Fans will debate for centuries whether or not Babe Ruth called his famous shot in game three of the 1932 World Series. But it is well known that the whole incident started as a result of a vicious bench-jockeying duel between the Yankees and the Cubs.

Toward the end of the season, Chicago had brought up ex-Yankee Mark Koenig to replace shortstop Billy Jurges. Koenig batted .353 and played a big part in Chicago's winning the pennant. When the Cubs only voted him a half-player share of the upcoming World Series winnings, the Yankees—and Ruth in particular—let them know they were a bunch of cheapskates and skinflints. As the Series

◇ YOU COULD LOOK IT UP ◇

• • • • • • • • • • • • • • • • • • •

"All players on a team shall wear uniforms identical in color, trim, and style.... No player shall wear ragged, frayed, or slit sleeves.... No player shall attach to his uniform tape or other material of a different color from his uniform.... No part of the uniform shall include a pattern that imitates or suggests the shape of a baseball.... Glass buttons and polished metal shall not be used on a uniform.... Shoes with pointed spikes similar to golf or track shoes shall not be worn.... No part of the uniform shall include patches or designs relating to commercial advertisements."

"The infield shall be graded so that the base lines and home plate are level."

"Players in uniform shall not address or mingle with spectators, nor sit in the stands before, during, or after a game."

"Players of opposing teams shall not fraternize at any time while in uniform."

"No manager, player, substitute, coach, trainer, or batboy shall at any time, whether from the bench, the coach's box or on the playing field, or elsewhere—
(1) Incite, or try to incite, by word or sign a demonstration by spectators;

• • •

◇ **YOU COULD LOOK IT UP** ◇

• • • • • • • • • • • • • • • • •

(2) Use language which will in any manner refer to or reflect upon opposing players, an umpire, or any spectator.''

''No fielder shall take a position in the batter's line of vision, and with deliberate unsportsmanlike intent, act in a manner to distract the batter.''

''Any runner is out when, after he has acquired legal possession of a base, he runs the bases in reverse order for the purpose of confusing the defense or making a travesty of the game.''·

''It is interference by a batter or runner when, with a runner on third base, the base coach leaves his box and acts in any manner to draw a throw by a fielder.''

• • •

began, the two teams were going at it hot and heavy from the dugouts. When the Yankees won the first two games, they became bolder and the Cubs more vindictive.

Ruth, considered a godlike legend today, was commonly referred to as ''the Big Baboon'' in his playing days. He was thirty-seven years old in 1932, and the Cub bench had been screaming that he was washed up, a potbelly who ''should be hitched to a wagon'' (as well as numerous unprintable insults). When Ruth clouted a homer in the first inning of game three, it riled the Cubs up even more. As he came to bat in the fifth inning, a lemon rolled to the plate. Ruth, an excellent bench jockey himself with a booming voice and vulgar wit, was giving it right back the entire time he was at bat. On a 2–2 count, he smashed the most mythical home run in baseball history.

The only existing film of the event—a 16mm home movie—clearly shows the Babe holding up his arm before the pitch was thrown. Perhaps he *was* pointing at the fence to tell the world where the next shot was going to go. But more likely, he was jawing with the Cubs and making mocking gestures, just as he did when he trotted around the bases. With heckling, like any psychological attack, bench jockeys run the risk of giving added motivation to their intended victims.

The night of Ruth's called shot, Judge Landis circulated a letter stating that any player using profanity would be fined five hundred dollars.

• • •

Psych Jobs

Non-fans frequently put down baseball, claiming it's a slow, boring game in which nothing seems to happen. What they don't appreciate is the psychodrama of baseball. The war going on between pitcher and batter. Between infielders and baserunners. Between catcher and base stealer. Between the two managers. There's a little story with each pitch that true fans understand and revel in. Psych jobs, decoys, fakeouts, and other deceptions are what make the game so fascinating.

In the 1972 World Series, the Oakland As did a job on Johnny Bench that he's probably still muttering about under his breath. It was the eighth inning of game three. Rollie Fingers was on the mound, with runners on second and third. Bench was up, with two strikes on him.

Catcher Gene Tenace and manager Dick Williams came out to chat with Fingers. Everyone in America knew they were considering intentionally walking Bench, especially when Williams pointed at first base. Tenace came back to the plate and held out his right hand, the usual signal for an intentional walk.

As prearranged, Fingers ignored the sign and threw the next pitch right down the middle. Bench was completely fooled, never getting the bat off his shoulder. Strike three.

Such elaborate tricks are not necessary for playing head games with an opponent. Before he reached the majors, Satchel Paige would sometimes have his outfielders leave the field. He would then proceed to strike out three overswinging hitters on nine straight pitches. Yankee fastballer Ryne Duren wore thick "Coke-bottle" eyeglasses and would intentionally heave his last warm-up pitch ten feet over the plate, making trembling hitters think he was both vision-impaired and wild.

"It helps if the hitter thinks you're a little crazy," notes Nolan Ryan.

Remember when Willie Mays used to run out from under his hat chasing a fly ball or stealing a base? It was a ruse. It wasn't until he retired that Mays revealed the hat was too big for his head. He wore it large on purpose to give the illusion that he was running faster than he actually was. (Bob Uecker claims he used to purposely knock his own hat off running to first for the same reason. But in Uecker's case, the speed *was* an illusion.)

Managers also play head games to get an edge. George Stallings motivated his Boston Braves to beat the Athletics in the 1914 World Series by telling the players that Connie Mack had refused to let them practice in Shibe Park. When somebody asked Earl Weaver if Cincinnati's artificial surface would bother his players in the 1970 World Series, he said cleverly, "The turf won't bother us as much as the white houses beyond centerfield in Baltimore will bother the Reds."

Pete Rose once psyched out the entire American League. Before the All-Star game in 1978, he got a batch of smaller, livelier Japanese baseballs and had the National League hitters use them during batting practice. The American League hitters watched dumbfounded as even lightweight hitters like Larry

Bowa sent the bogus balls over the walls. When the AL got their chance with regulation balls, they were already psyched out and lost the game for the fifteenth time in sixteen years.

Sitting in the stands or watching TV, we rarely get to see the subtle fakery between players that doesn't show up in the box score.

If a good outfielder knows he has no chance to catch a fly ball, he'll pretend he's got it all the way, so baserunners will stop in their tracks. Infielders have the best opportunity to be decoys. If a baserunner doesn't quite follow the batted ball, savvy infielders can mess with their minds. Bobby Grich used to pretend easy pop-ups were grounders so the runner would slide stupidly into the next base instead of scampering back to where he was. Shortstop Fred Stanley used to tell incoming runners the ball had been grounded foul, and sometimes they'd stop and go back to first before realizing Stanley had deked them into a double play.

When there's a runner on second, Chicago shortstop Ozzie Guillen likes to toss a handful of dirt near his right foot. When the runner looks right, Guillen sneaks in left and takes a pickoff throw. Devious.

The recent rash of cheating has added a new form of psyching to the game. Continually confiscating a player's bat (as Whitey Herzog did to Howard Johnson) not only unnerves him, but also soils his reputation. Some hitters develop ''hydrophobia''—fear of the spitball. They worry so much about illegal pitches that they don't concentrate on hitting. Pitchers have gone so far as to spread rumors about themselves cheating so opposing batters have something else to worry about.

Putting one over on the umpire can be just as satisfying and effective as tricking the other team. Most players wear tight-fitting uniforms now, but in past decades they wore them baggy and perfected the art form of pretending to get hit by the pitch. Ron Hunt, Minnie Minoso, and other league-leading hit batters knew to roll with those inside pitches and scamper to first on anything close. The umpire will usually give you the benefit of the doubt, especially if you toss your bat away angrily, curse in pain, and shout menacingly at the pitcher. In 1971, Hunt was hit by a pitch in one out of every ten times he came to the plate.

Sometimes, the trick works even on foul balls. "You'd fall down on your belly, and while you were down you'd try to make a red spot by squeezing your hand or something," remembers Fred Snodgrass of his days with the Giants. "If you had a good red spot there, the umpire might believe it hit you rather than the bat."

A catcher (like Bob Boone) can fool the ump by ever-so-slightly moving his glove into the strike zone on borderline pitches. First basemen (like Gil Hodges) do it by stepping gracefully off the bag a millisecond before the ball arrives on close plays. Shortstops and second basemen do it by making the pivot on a double-play ball without bothering to tag second base. This is called a "phantom double play," and Julian Javier used to be so good at it that his nickname was "the Phantom."

Short guys go into a deep crouch to make their strike zone smaller. Willie Mays says that in his rookie season Leo Durocher gave him this piece of valuable career advice: "When you put on your pants, pull them up higher. They were so low out there today, the umpires thought the strike zone went all the way down to your ankles."

The story is told that Sadie McMahon was pitching for the Baltimore Orioles in the days before night games, and darkness was descending on the field. He had two strikes on a batter and wanted to get things over with. So instead of pitching the ball, McMahon went through the *motion* of pitching and his catcher Wilbert Robinson smacked his fist into the glove, as if he had caught the ball.

"Three strikes! Yer out!" cried the umpire.

Legend has it that the irate batter responded, "What are you, crazy?! That ball was two feet outside!"

Superstitions and Head Games

As Yogi Berra once astutely noted, 90 percent of baseball is mental and the other half is physical. Since the earliest days of the game, players have been trying to play head games with *themselves* to improve the quality of their performance.

Ballplayers are notoriously superstitious. Willie Mays always made it a point to touch second base on his way to or from the outfield, and Jackie Robinson never stepped into the batter's box until the catcher was in position. Wade Boggs, the best hitter in the game today, isn't confident enough of his own ability to go a day without eating chicken. After one hitless game, Minnie Minoso took a shower with his uniform on to wash away any evil spirits. He got three hits the next game and eight of his teammates jumped into the shower fully clothed.

Tap dancer Bill ''Bojangles'' Robinson was a big Yankee fan. Whenever the team was coming into a big series, he would pull out a vial of his secret ''goofer'' dust, do a dance, and sprinkle the stuff over the team's bats and gloves. Babe Ruth said that on one occasion the Yankees went into a hitting frenzy after Lou Gehrig's mother sent a jar of pickled eels to the clubhouse. After that, the team couldn't go out on the field without a few bites of the stuff.

In these more enlightened times, players don't need to rely on cheap gimmicks such as superstition. Now they rely on *expensive* gimmicks like hypnosis, visualization, and transcendental meditation. The Phillies installed a ''mood room'' in the basement of Veterans Stadium where Steve Carlton, in particular, would get his head together.

Harvey Misel, a man who once tried to market an electric rodent repeller, attracted two hundred major league clients to his hypnosis practice, including Rod Carew, Tony Oliva, George Brett, and the entire 1983 Chicago White Sox. Earl Weaver knows how to hypnotize people and says hypnosis helped Maury

Wills conquer his fear of flying and Paul Blair his fear of curveballs.

Leon Durham used a much less expensive method to improve his hitting. Before each season, his mother would pray over his bats.

One day in 1911, a man named Charles Faust walked up to manager John McGraw and said a fortune-teller had told him the New York Giants would win the pennant if he joined the team. McGraw, who was so superstitious that he'd hire men to ride past the Giants' hotel with a load of barrels for good luck, signed Faust up. He couldn't play for beans, but he came out to the ballpark, joined the team for road trips, and warmed up every day as if he were a real player.

Maybe it was just a coincidence, but the Giants *did* finish first in 1911. Because of this success, Faust was asked back in 1912 and the Giants won again. The same thing happened in 1913.

Interestingly, that winter Charles Victory Faust died, and for the next three years the Giants came in second, eighth, and fourth. Makes you wonder.

Performance-Enhancing Pharmaceuticals

Baseball has had its problems with cocaine, but most agree that its use is for recreation, not for getting an edge in the game. When ballplayers decide they need a little more pop in their swing or a few more MPH on their fastball, they usually grab some dextroamphetamine sulphate—or "greenies," as they're more popularly called.

Greenies are uppers that, whether or not they make you play better, at least make you *feel* like you're playing better. They're banned in clubhouses, but players get them from doctor friends or in the Dominican Republic while playing winter ball. The use of greenies was first revealed in Jim Bouton's *Ball Four*, where it was reported that more than half of all players used them.

Professional athletes are so used to routinely popping analgesics, uppers, downers, and anti-inflammatory drugs that it's remarkable there have only been a few serious drug problems in baseball.

The rewards of winning and putting up big numbers are incredible, and the fact that players are willing to risk their health is perhaps the best indication of how important it is to win at all costs. When Don Drysdale damaged his shoulder, he was so doped up with painkillers that he could barely read the scoreboard, much less see a line drive coming at him. Rumors have recently circulated about players taking anabolic steroids, even though they have been linked to impotence and sterility. Some players have even experimented with dimethylsulfoxide—D.M.S.O.—despite the fact that doctors say it has no medical use and rumors say it can make a man go blind.

"If you had a pill that would guarantee a pitcher twenty wins but might take five years off his life," claims Bouton, "he'd take it."

Cheating by Managers

When a ballplayer doesn't win, he can defend himself at contract time by bringing up his impressive statistics, his injuries, his rotten teammates, or any number of other excuses. When a manager doesn't win, there's no defense. He gets fired. So managers have an even bigger incentive for cheating than the players do. When his team hit foul pops into the Montreal dugout, Gene Mauch went so far as to smack the ball out of the opposing catcher's glove.

Earl Weaver tells a story about Paul Richards, who managed the Baltimore Orioles before the Weaver years. Richards had a hard-hitting minor leaguer on the roster named Chuck Hinton, who was likely to be snapped up by one of the expansion teams in 1961. To prevent that from happening, Richards instructed Hinton to run into the left-field wall chasing a fungo, fall down, and pretend to be seriously injured. Presumably, word would get around that Hinton was damaged goods and nobody would choose him. (The trick backfired. Hinton *was* chosen and hit .310 with seventeen homers for the Washington Senators in 1962.)

Richards is also credited with creating the "elephant glove" in 1958. Baltimore catchers were having a helluva time with Hoyt Wilhelm's knuckleball, so Richards went to Wilson Sporting Goods and had them construct a glove that looked to be about the size of a garbage can cover. At the time, nobody had bothered writing a rule that limited the size of a fielder's glove. Since then, somebody has; now catcher's gloves cannot have a circumference of more than thirty-eight inches.

Minnesota Twins manager Tom Trebelhorn was nabbed in 1988, and he didn't even mean to cheat. With both a Yount (Robin) and a Young (Mike) in his batting order, one day Trebelhorn accidentally wrote out his lineup card with "Y-O-U-N-T" in both the third and fifth positions. Tiger manager Sparky Anderson brought this to the attention of the umpires, who ruled that *anyone* named Yount was out of the game. Probably to ease his embarrassment, Trebelhorn argued with the umpires, but in short order *he* was thrown out of the game as well.

But then, getting thrown out of a game isn't the worst thing in the world to happen to a manager, especially in these days of modern electronics. Earl Weaver says he had a closed-circuit TV and a phone line to the dugout in his office, though he never admitted actually using the equipment to manage after being ejected from a game.

"You can go down into the clubhouse, or the runway, and manage a game from there," Roger Craig revealed in his *Playboy* interview. "The umpires know it, but there's nothin' they can do. And these days, you've got these remote telephones, all those walkie-talkies.''

The high-tech isn't even necessary. When Leo Durocher got thrown out of a game (a fairly regular event), he would go up to the press box and relay his signs through Barney Kremenko, a writer with the *New York Journal-American*.

According to Duke Snider, Chuck Dressen found a simple way to manage the Dodgers after getting thrown out of a game. He put on a fake mustache and glasses and joined the grounds-keeping crew for the rest of the afternoon.

Cheating by Owners

You can have your Ted Turner (who once sent his manager on a scouting mission and managed the team himself). You can have your Ray Kroc (who once got on the P.A. system and told the fans, ''I've never seen such stupid ballplaying in all my life''). You can have your George Steinbrenner (don't even ask). The two most outrageous team owners were Bill Veeck and Charlie Finley. Both were mischievous, almost lovable cheaters.

In the early sixties, Finley claimed the Yankees won the pennant every year because of their short right-field fence. He erected a ''pennant porch'' in Kansas City Municipal Stadium's right field to shorten the distance and bring it in line with Yankee Stadium. Commissioner Ford Frick had it removed.

When he couldn't actually change the distances, Finley switched tactics and altered all the numbers on the fences indicating how far they were from the plate. If he added twenty feet to each number, he reasoned, his pitchers would have more confidence. A sportswriter foiled the trick by getting down on his hands and knees and measuring the outfield distances with a tape measure.

But that's nothing. Bill Veeck simply moved the fences.

When he owned the Indians, Veeck had six sets of sockets sunk into the outfield of Cleveland Municipal Stadium at different distances. Depending on which team was coming to town, he would have the fences moved in or out the night before a game. Veeck was also known to have home plate dug up and moved forward or back. In the late thirties, he sold fans small pocket mirrors to shine in the eyes of enemy batters.

Both men were colorful innovators who would do anything to drag fans into the ballpark. It was Veeck who invented the exploding scoreboard. It was Veeck who originally put the ivy up in Wrigley Field, and was the first to put the players' names on the backs of their uniforms. Veeck scheduled games at 8:30 A.M. to bring in shift workers, and he gave them free milk and cornflakes to munch during the game. He was also responsible for the infamous "Disco Demolition Night" and will always be remembered as the guy who let a midget come to bat in a major league game.

Veeck's cleverest promotion was "Grandstand Manager's Day" on August 24, 1951, when he owned the St. Louis Browns. Five hundred fans were given placards with the word "YES" on them, and another five hundred received "NO" placards. At strategic points in the game, the fans were polled, "Should we walk him?" "Bring the infield in?" "Bunt?" and other crucial managerial decisions. In each situation the majority ruled and the Brownies would carry out the fans' wishes.

It worked, too. The Browns won 5–3. A little-known fact is that Connie Mack was at the stadium that day, and he held up a "YES" sign several times.

Charlie Finley specialized in the outrageous, with such innovations as Day-Glo orange baseballs, designated runners, multicolored uniforms, "Bald-headed Men's Day," greased-pig chases before games, air tubes to dust off home plate, and a mechanical rabbit named Harvey who brought fresh balls to the umpires in his paws. Finley, who had a special fondness for animals, put a flock of sheep beyond the right-field fence, a zoo in left, and the team mascot was a mule named, naturally, Charlie O.

They just don't make owners like these anymore. When medical problems required Veeck to have his leg removed, he threw a "Post-Amputation Party" and danced the night away on his wooden prosthesis.

Cheating by Fans

When you're sitting behind a barrier in foul territory, there's not a whole lot you can do to influence the outcome of a baseball game. But that has never stopped fans from trying. The word "fan," it should be remembered, is a shortened form of "fanatic."

When we think back to those carefree, halcyon days of baseball yesteryear, we rarely recall the game in 1897 when a beer stein sailed out of the stands and hit the umpire. Like any red-blooded American, he heaved it back, and it knocked a local fireman unconscious. Riots were common in those days, sometimes serious enough that hoses were turned on the fans. And this was in the days before fans knew how to perform for television cameras.

During the "dead-ball era" there was no need for outfield fences, and fans were allowed to stand right in the back of the field. Clark Griffith recalled an incident when a long drive was hit into a crowd of fans and the hitter was awarded a home run after a fan ran off with the ball. Cub fans in those days were required to stand behind a rope in the outfield. Naturally, they would push the rope forward when the Cubs were at bat and move back when the visiting team came to the plate.

Poor Fred Snodgrass usually gets the blame for his "$100,000 muff" that cost the Giants the 1912 World Series. With the Giants ahead 2–1 in the tenth inning, Snodgrass was foolish enough to be running after a fly ball at the exact same moment that a bottle was flying through the air in his general direction. Distracted, he missed the ball, the Red Sox rallied, and won the Series.

Some fans apparently believe throwing things is at least as effective as chanting "Darrrrr-ylllll!" to annoy opposing players. Dave Parker has been hit by a bag of nuts and bolts; Pete Rose has been hit on the head with a souvenir bat. Chris Chambliss had a steel-tipped dart whiz past his head and Wally Joyner was grazed by a flying knife at Yankee Stadium. A fan lobbed a cherry bomb into the Minnesota dugout a few years back, injuring several players. Some guys won't go out on the field without a batting helmet. It's almost a status symbol. The bigger the star, the more interesting the objects that are hurled at him.

"Over the years I've had fruit thrown at me, beer dumped in my face and hit in the back by a baseball fired from the bleachers," claims Dave Winfield. "In Yankee Stadium I was in the outfield just minding my own business when suddenly— *shoop!*—an arrow pierced the ground next to me. Metal tip and everything. Inches into the ground. No way it could have gotten there without a bow. A bow? How did someone get a bow into Yankee Stadium?"

The Cleveland management had a bright idea in 1974. They held a "Beer Night" promotion and sold suds for ten cents a glass. After about 600,000 ounces had been consumed, the fans attacked Texas outfielder Jeff Burroughs with chairs. His teammates rushed out on the field wielding their bats. Nine fans were arrested, umpire Nestor Chylak was bloodied, and the game was forfeited to the Rangers.

Usually, fans are content to stay in their seats and hurl verbal abuse. Winfield says the fans in New York, Oakland, Chicago, and Boston are the roughest on opponents, and the older, more intimate stadiums like Fenway Park and Wrigley Field amplify the effect of the crowd.

There certainly is a home-field advantage in baseball. Almost every team has a better record at home than on the road, and at least part of this can be attributed to its fans. Teams know the power of the crowd. A woman in St. Louis named Mary Ott had such an obnoxious voice that she was given a free pass to Cardinals games in the hope that she would use her talents against opponents. A Philadelphia man named Pete Adelis was so annoying that he was banned for life from Ebbets Field in Brooklyn. Adelis, known as "the Iron Lung of Shibe Park," was actually brought to Yankee Stadium to harass the Cleveland Indians in the fifties.

When the fans start becoming free agents, you know baseball is a serious business.

Cheating by Umpires!

Yes, sports fans. Even *umpires*— the defenders of the integrity of baseball—had been known to play by their own rule book on occasion.

Catfish Hunter says that during his rookie season, veteran umpire Ed Runge taught him a lesson he never forgot. The first game Hunter pitched with Runge behind the plate, Catfish couldn't get a break. He threw right down the middle and Runge inexplicably called ball after ball. Hunter kept his cool and didn't say a word in protest.

A few weeks later the two bumped into each other before a game and Runge said, "I see you don't argue with umpires, kid."

"From then on," Catfish explains, "I was a card-carrying member of the Ed Runge Club. Anything close was a strike."

Umpires will rarely admit it, but players such as Hunter who earn their respect get the benefit of the doubt in close calls. The great hurlers—like Jim Palmer and Tom Seaver—got borderline pitches called strikes simply because they'd earned reputations as masters of their craft. Nolan Ryan, on the other hand, always had a reputation for being wild and rarely got close calls in his favor.

Superior hitters—Ted Williams and Wade Boggs, for example, who are known for their knowledge of the strike zone—are said to be allowed four strikes in every turn at bat. Consciously or subconsciously, the umpires figure that if Boggs didn't swing at a close pitch, it must not have been a strike. Ted Williams never argued with umpires, and even went to their dressing rooms at the end of each season to thank them for their hard work all year.

Bill Lee says that when he pitched to an aging Al Kaline, he threw five straight strikes, but Kaline drew a walk. When Lee complained to the home-plate umpire, he was told, "Son, Mr. Kaline will let you know it's a strike by doubling off the wall."

There are other reasons why umpires will sometimes give a guy a break. If a rookie hitter is from the umpire's hometown, his strike zone may shrink a few inches. If the umpire blows a call and knows it, he may try to make it up to the guy the next time he has a chance. In an effort to be fair, an umpire will sometimes cheat.

Or sometimes they'll do it just for the fun of it. Jay Johnstone says that he had a plane to catch on the last day of one season, so before the game he asked umpire Bill Haller to eject him early. Haller said he couldn't do that, but when Johnstone got on base in the third inning and started jawing about balks, Haller obligingly threw him out.

The famous umpire Jocko Conlan actually let a hitter umpire *himself* for one pitch. Richie Ashburn was at the plate and complained about one of Conlan's strike calls. "Okay," said Conlan. "*You* call the next pitch."

The pitch came in and Conlan said nothing. Ashburn turned around and hesitatingly said, "Strike?" Conlan shot up his arm and indicated strike. With that, Conlan dusted off the plate and said to Ashburn, "Richie, you just had the only chance in the history of baseball to hit and umpire at the same time. And you blew it.''

Umpires don't like to be shown up. If the pitcher or batter starts waving his arms around and arguing after a close pitch, many umpires will hold it against him in the future. Just like ballplayers, the umpires are part of the show, and they want to look good out there. Some umpires don't care what four-letter words you say to them, as long as you don't turn around, face them, and show the crowd you think they blew the call.

For the same reason, if the catcher sets up an inch off the outside corner and the pitch hits his glove perfectly, umpires will frequently call the pitch a strike even though they know it's a ball. If the umpire did otherwise, he would look like he missed the call. Besides, the pitcher had demonstrated pinpoint control, which certainly counts for something in this game.

If umpires rarely reverse a decision about a play, what's the point of arguing a call? Because an intimidating display by a player or manager will sometimes be the difference between a safe or out call the *next* time there's a close play. The squeaky wheel, as they say, gets the grease.

Some umpires are simply mean. Ozzie Smith is convinced that after he became a star and started pulling down two million dollars a year, the umpires made it harder on him. ''Since my contract, my strike zone has all of a sudden become a lot larger,'' claims Ozzie. ''I have to think a lot of umpires are trying to call me out just so they can show me that they're boss.''

Earl Weaver says that if an umpire is determined to throw you out of a game, he will get so close to you in an argument that he'll hit the bill of your hat. When it falls off, he will claim you bumped him and give you the thumb. Bill Klem, the most famous of all baseball umpires, once hauled off and belted Boston manager Fred Tenney because Tenney ''felt my pockets for balls'' after a game.

All of this is not meant to show that umpires necessarily cheat, but that they are human beings—with all the flaws and idiosyncrasies that come with the species.

In 1972, Federal agents raided the home of a man who was eventually charged with bookmaking, conspiracy, and maintaining a gambling establishment. One thing they found in the man's possession was an address book with the names of eleven major league umpires in it. No charges were ever leveled and no corruption was uncovered. Considering the small amount of money umpires earn and the tremendous amount of money that is at stake in baseball, it is remarkable that there has never been a scandal involving an umpire in the one hundred and forty years of baseball's history.

• • • Ty Cobb • • •

There's no evidence proving the popular legend that Ty Cobb sharpened his spikes in order to slice up infielders who dared get in his way. He is frequently hailed as the most aggressive player in baseball's history, but Cobb gets little credit for the psychological and strategic genius he displayed to get an edge.

When he reached first, Cobb would kick at the bag. It wasn't a nervous habit; he wanted to move it a few inches closer to second base so he could get back more easily on pickoff attempts. When he took off and slid into the next base, Cobb perfected the technique of tracking the infielder's eyes as they watched the ball. This way, Cobb could direct his slide so the ball would hit *him* instead of the fielder's glove.

Cobb's career span (1905–1928) almost perfectly matched Walter Johnson's (1907–1927), and he pulled a psych job on Johnson the entire time. Knowing that Johnson was afraid his fastball might kill a man, Cobb would crowd the plate and force him to work the outside corner. (Johnson still hit 208 batters, a record in this century.)

"I even practiced limping," Cobb once said. "It's a great help to stumble deliberately at first base and come up lame, or to seem to be hurt by your slide. If your act is good enough, the pitcher and catcher relax and it's no trick at all to steal second."

Cobb was so effective on the basepaths that the Cleveland Indians devised an offbeat trick play to stop him. When he tried to steal second, the catcher would deliberately throw the ball into centerfield. This would prompt Cobb to continue to third. The centerfielder would intentionally bobble the ball. When Cobb broke for home, the centerfielder would throw him out at the plate by a mile.

On paper, anyway. The problem was, Cobb always beat the throw, and Cleveland gave up on the trick play.

Of course, Cobb wasn't merely a genius. He was also just plain mean. He once stormed into the stands and beat up a heckler, who happened to have only one arm. Another time, fans attacked him and knifed him in the back. After he bloodied Frank "Home Run" Baker with a slide in 1909, he received thirteen letters threatening to kill him at the next game against Philadelphia.

When Cobb passed away in 1961, only three baseball people showed up to pay their respects. One of his obituaries read, "The only difference now is that he is a bad guy who is dead."

Even in the years when most men are mellowing, Cobb played the game as he always had. While coaching an all-star high-school game at the end of his life, Cobb gave a long, serious talk to the players about the importance of sportsmanship. When the players began their workout, he pulled the catcher aside and gave him a little tip: "Remember, just before the batter swings, flip a little dirt in his eye."

• • •

• • • Rogers Hornsby • • •

"If a big-league player doesn't like cutting the corners or playing with 'cheaters,' then he's as much out of place as a missionary in Russia," wrote Hall of Famer Rogers Hornsby in his autobiography *My War with Baseball*. Hornsby, whose player/manager career stretched all the way from 1915 to 1959, pretty much cut loose in the book. It was published just before he passed away in 1963.

"I've 'cheated' or watched someone on my team 'cheat' in practically every game," he wrote. "Ballplayers are always trying to beat the rules."

As a hitter, Hornsby didn't need any extra help (lifetime average: .358). But in the field he took every edge he could get. "When I played second base," he wrote, "I used to trip, kick, elbow or spike anybody I could."

It is in the pitching, of course, where cheating thrives. According to Hornsby, 95 percent of the pitchers in baseball throw illegal pitches. As a manager, he saw at least one of the members of his staff file his thumbnails to a point in order to cut the ball. Another chewed coffee grounds (yuck!) and dropped them into the seams.

None of this bothered Hornsby morally; he indicated clearly that he believed cheating to be a legitimate part of the game and honestly looked down on players who refused to practice rule bending.

"Pitchers who don't want to 'cheat' to win just don't fit into a winning organization," he said.

It wasn't Bill Mazeroski's dramatic ninth-inning home run that beat the Yankees in the 1960 World Series, according to Hornsby. It was the Pittsburgh groundskeeper. Over the years, the Pirates signed many hitters who slashed *down* at the ball, so Forbes Field was rolled as hard as a rock to speed up ground balls and cause bad hops.

"Sometimes the ball shoots so crazy that you couldn't field it with a bushel basket," wrote Hornsby.

The inning before Mazeroski's homer, Bill Virdon hit a shot that bounced up off the dirt and smashed Yankee shortstop Tony Kubek in the throat.* The Pirates converted the break into three runs, setting the stage for Maz to win it in the ninth.

The most startling revelation that Hornsby offered in *My War with Baseball* was the skullduggery of Frank Lane, an executive with the Cleveland Indians. Lane took cheating to a creative level that has never been equaled before or since. Hornsby claims that before one very hot Fourth of July doubleheader, Lane put an air conditioner in the Cleveland dugout and a *heater* in the dugout of the visiting team!

Lane's genius may have crossed the line into sadism after he left Cleveland to work for the Kansas City Athletics. If Hornsby is to be believed, Lane made it a point *not* to put a toilet in the visiting team's clubhouse. That's one way to avoid extra-inning games.

"Cheating started when they threw out the first ball in the first game ever played," claimed Rogers Hornsby, "and it's been going on ever since."

• • •

* At the time there was speculation that Kubek would never speak again, a prediction that has been proven to be ironically untrue.

◇ **THEY SAID IT** ◇

· · · · · · · · · · · · · · · · · ·

"I must have helped Willie Mays to at least another twenty-five homers in his career by letting him know what pitch was coming."

—*Wes Westrum, Giants coach*

"Stanky couldn't hit, run, or field. He couldn't do anything except beat you. He would sit on you at second base to keep you there. He would pull on your shirt, step on you. . . . When he got on base he immediately filled his hands with dirt. . . . He wanted something to throw in the second baseman's face."

—*Alvin Dark*

"Emil Lajong did a backward flip whenever he located a cross-eyed fan in the stands. . . . Pop sometimes stroked a rabbit's foot. Red Blow never changed his clothes during a 'winning streak,' and Flores secretly touched his genitals whenever a bird flew over his head."

—*Bernard Malamud*, The Natural

"You lose your concentration when [fans] try to hit you on the head with a bottle or try to put your eye out with an ice cube."

—*Pete Rose*

· · ·

The Physics of Cheating

"Clearly, a pitcher who wished to use the drag crisis to advantage would like to be able to change the aerodynamic properties of the baseball so that different pitches could be affected by entirely different drag curves."

> —Dr. Cliff Frohlich, Institute for Geophysics, University of Texas, in "Aerodynamic Drag Crisis and Its Possible Effect on the Flight of Baseballs," *The American Journal of Physics*

Why would a ball with a scuff mark or dab of grease behave more erratically than a clean ball? Why would a bat filled with cork drive a ball farther than one made of solid wood? Why is so much perfectly good sporting equipment being mutilated by major league baseball players?

Ballplayers, who usually don't make it past high school, understand that the laws of gravity, ballistics, and aerodynamics can be tinkered with to gain an edge in their game. But to find out *why*, you've got to go to a professional baseball physicist.

Pete Brancazio is a guy sports announcers love to hate. The Brooklyn College physics professor and author of *Sport Science* has the audacity to tell the baseball establishment it would violate Newton's Second Law for a fastball to rise or for a peg from third to travel on a straight, horizontal plane to first base. In reality, Brancazio says, any projectile begins dropping the instant it leaves the hand, bat, or gun. Even a 100 MPH fastball will drop two feet, two inches on its way to the plate.

"I'm sitting at home watching a ballgame and minding my own business when I hear Tim McCarver call me an idiot," says Brancazio, who neither looks nor sounds like a physicist. "I mean, what the hell do announcers know about physics? At least I've *played* baseball."

Nobody ever won a Nobel Prize for putting a hardball in a wind tunnel. Like sex, sports has been considered a legitimate topic for study by scientists only recently. There are no journals, funding agencies, or organizations that encourage research. Only on rare occasions does an article like "Effect of Spin and Speed on the Lateral Deflection of a Baseball" worm its way into *The American Journal of Physics*. There are only about five physicists who regularly publish scholarly research papers on baseball. But if you want to know why guys are corking, spitting, and scuffing, Pete Brancazio is the guy to see.

Why Does a Corked Bat Work?

"Stuffing Super Balls in your bat is absolute nonsense," snorts Brancazio, referring to the 1974 incident when Graig Nettles's bat shattered and balls bounced around the infield. He chuckles at the theory that a hollowed-out bat with rubber inside would somehow expand explosively upon impact with the ball.

Casual observers often make the assumption that illegal bats are effective because the cork or other springy substance embedded inside makes the bat bouncier. In reality, putting a bouncy material against the ball is the *opposite* of what a batter wants to do. When two objects collide, energy is transferred from one object to the other. In causing the collision between bat and ball, the goal is to transfer energy to the ball and *not* to the bat.

The harder the surface of the bat, the better. In fact, high-speed photos of a bat hitting a ball show that a wooden bat is deformed hardly at all in the collision, but the baseball is crushed to nearly half its size. If bouncier bats made baseballs travel farther, bats would be made of rubber. The force that a bat puts on a ball has nothing to do with what's inside it.

What actually happens with a corked bat is much simpler—hollowing out the bat makes it *lighter*. Cork is one-third the weight of wood. Tampering with the wood doesn't put more bang in your bat; it just makes it possible to swing it faster and delay your decision to swing at a pitch a millisecond or two longer.

The faster a bat is moving when it strikes a ball, the more force it imparts and the farther the ball will travel. *Bat speed is the most important factor in hitting the ball far.* (Duke Snider's swing was once measured at 115 miles per hour.) The lighter the bat, the farther the ball is going to go. It's as simple as that.

If you could knock off six ounces from a 32-ounce bat, bat speed would be increased 2.5 percent and the ball would carry an extra fifteen to twenty feet on a fly, according to a study by one of Brancazio's colleagues, Dr. Robert Watts of Tulane University. In fact, according to Brancazio's calculations of bat speed and hitting distance, the optimum bat weight is a toothpick-light 20 ounces.

When asked why so many batters insist on using heavy bats, Pete Brancazio, a true Brooklynite, offers a simple explanation: "Because they're stupid."

But if a lighter bat makes a better hitting instrument, why bother with the mess and fuss of drilling holes? Why not just select a lighter bat from the bat rack?

Because a lighter bat is a smaller bat. To make a 34-ounce piece of solid wood into 32 ounces *legally*, it stands to reason that you've got to cut two ounces off somewhere. If you cut them off one of the ends, it makes the bat shorter. If you shave them off the barrel, it makes the bat thinner. In either case, you end up with a smaller, less effective weapon.

That 20-ounce bat may be perfect according to a computer, but it's simply too small to be usable. (Besides, all the guys on the team would laugh.) An even more perfect idealized bat would be one that is flexible enough to *whip* at the ball, but size and shape requirements make it difficult to build much flexibility into wood.

So hitters face a tradeoff: A heavy bat transfers more momentum to the ball and has a larger hitting surface, but it's harder to accelerate and takes longer to get around. A lighter bat swings faster, but you give up hitting surface, so there is less margin for error when you swing.

"Bat speed is more important a consideration than weight," claims Brancazio, who has worked all this out on his TRS-80 Model III computer. "It's more effective to swing the lightest bat you can."

Without really knowing why, for decades players have been swinging weighted bats in the on-deck circle to make their real bat feel lighter when they step to the plate. Ty Cobb used to put lead weights in his shoes during spring training to make him run faster on Opening Day. Lighter is truly better. We can only speculate how many home runs Babe Ruth would have hit had he known about the benefit of using a lighter bat in his glory years.

A New Way to Cheat

So how do you get quick bat speed without sacrificing hitting surface? Well, one way is by cheating. With a corked bat, the hitter has it both ways—the bat is lighter, and it still has its large hitting surface.

Some observers have pointed out that a hitter would have an even *lighter* bat if he hollowed it out and left the insides *empty*. Cork only adds to the weight. True, but such a bat is more likely to crack, and it makes a distinctive hollow sound when it strikes the ball.

There is one other way for the hitter to get bat speed without sacrificing hitting surface—with an aluminum bat. These bats are hollow, so they can be light. They can also be made in any length and thickness.

Aluminum bats aren't allowed in professional baseball, and would certainly revolutionize the game if they were. Former National League batting champ Dick Groat testified in U.S. District Court that aluminum bats would turn spray hitters into sluggers and make it common for major league players to hit sixty to seventy home runs a season. A potential problem is that kids of today are growing up using aluminum bats and then have to switch to wood when they get to pro ball. In fact, until he signed his bonus, slugger Kirk Gibson of the Dodgers had never swung anything but an aluminum bat.

Pete Brancazio says that aluminum and corked bats have another advantage over legal bats, which is that they have a larger "sweet spot." Because the barrel is hollow, the center of gravity is closer to the hands. Hitters have noticed. "I've hit with an aluminum bat—and what a joy it is," says New York Mets star Keith Hernandez. "You can't get jammed. A ball hit on the hands is still a line drive."

"I've got this idea I'm going to start playing around with," Dr. Brancazio whispers, as if Fay Vincent were hiding in the next office. "You take a wooden bat and you stick a lead disk on the knob under your hands. The mathematics work out that if you weight the handle of the bat, you make a wooden bat more like an aluminum bat and you should get better hitting response."

Listening, umpires?

The funny thing about illegal bats is that it isn't even clear that they *do anything*. Hillerich & Bradsby, makers of the Louisville Slugger, ran some tests for the commissioner's office in which hollowed-out bats were filled with Styrofoam. They hit baseballs with the doctored bats and recorded the distances.

"In general, it did not have a great deal of effect on performance," says H&B vice president of technical services George Manning. Hillerich & Bradsby also found that if more than two ounces were gouged out of a bat, the wood was weakened and broke very easily. It's possible that the advantage of using a doctored bat is mostly psychological.

According to Brancazio, a "dimple" cut into the end of the bat's barrel trims off just as much weight as corking does, and is perfectly legal. These "teacupped" bats were invented in 1936, but didn't become popular until Lou Brock started using one in the seventies. It is also legal to shave wood off the handle of the bat in order to make it lighter without losing hitting surface. Either way, Brancazio claims, making the bat lighter only adds six or seven feet to the distance a ball will travel.

Of course, how many times have we seen fly-ball outs that were six or seven feet short of being home runs?

The effectiveness of a corked bat may be debatable, but an illegally *grooved* bat can be a real help to a hitter because it increases the amount of backspin on the ball. Golfers are familiar with this effect. As the ball spins backward at 8,000 RPM off the grooved club, the irregular surface creates aerodynamic lift and the ball sails. The same thing happens with a baseball if grooves have been sliced into the surface of the bat.

The amount of backspin is affected by how much friction there is in the collision between bat and ball. Grooves create friction, and so would a sticky substance like pine tar, which is why George Brett's famous bat was ruled illegal. Tulane University mechanical engineer Robert Watts has determined that if .5 percent of all the energy transferred to the ball goes to making it spin, a fly ball will travel forty feet farther than it would if it weren't spinning.

For some strange reason, hitters remain convinced that corking works wonders, but we very rarely hear about players cheating by grooving their bats.

Why Does a Curve Curve?

To understand why a scuffball, spitball, or other illegal pitch behaves erratically, it's necessary to understand what would make a ball flying through the air deviate from a normal path in the first place.

Popular legend credits invention of the curveball to Hall of Famer Candy Cummings, who was inspired in the summer of 1863 when he noticed he could throw a clamshell and make it veer off course. "What a wonderful thing it would be if I could make a baseball curve like that!" he rhapsodized.

Fourteen years later, Cummings still hadn't convinced the world. "It is absurd to say that any man could throw a ball other than in a straight line," claimed Colonel J. B. Joyce, manager of the Cincinnati Red Stockings. Despite the fact that men had been tossing benders, jughandles, and pretzel curves for decades, until recent years many believed that what ballplayers called a curveball was just an illusion.

In 1941, *Life* magazine photographers armed with high-speed strobes attempted to settle the controversy by photographing the curveball in flight. Their conclusion was that "this stand-by of baseball is, after all, only an optical illusion." In 1952, a Canadian named Ernest Lowry was so incensed about the curveball "hoax" being foisted on youth that he suggested legal proceedings.

Life eventually repeated the test and photographically captured the curve in all its glory. But the controversy still didn't go away. As recently as 1960, *Newsweek* ran an article entitled "Does a Curve Curve?"

Today, physicists are quick to point out that a curveball *does* curve, but there is some debate as to whether or not a pitch can break *sharply*. Basically, the argument goes like this:

Physicists: "Pitches curve, they don't break. It's an optical illusion, kind of like watching an approaching train. In the distance, it seems to be moving slowly, but when it is near, it looks much faster."

Ballplayers: "Bull. Step to the plate and try to hit one, weenie."

Given the fact that a baseball can, in fact, curve, the question becomes "Why?" Randy Miller of the Orioles once semi-seriously hypothesized that curves were a result of the earth's turning beneath them. The truth is, there are two legal ways to make a baseball curve:

(1) Spin it.
(2) Don't spin it.

In other words, it's almost impossible *not* to throw a curve of some sort. Even a fastball is a curveball. Dwight Gooden holds his fastball across the seams to make it ride up, and he holds it *with* the seams if he wants lateral movement. Every power pitcher wants his fastball to move.

Spinning is the key. Most pitches spin when you throw them. A good fastball, slider, or curve can rotate as many as thirty revolutions per second, or sixteen complete turns on its way to the plate. Back in 1665, twenty-three-year-old Isaac Newton (who might have had a helluva curve had baseball been invented), noted that a tennis ball was affected when thrown or hit with a spin.

Anyone who has stuck a hand out a car window on the highway can appreciate the forces acting on a pitched baseball. The flow of air rushing by can't go through the ball, just as it can't go through your hand, so it is forced to go above or below it. If the ball didn't spin and was perfectly smooth like a billiard ball, the "wake" of air moving past it would be identical at the top and bottom and it would just slow the ball down rather than curve it.

But when a ball spins, the flow of air around it becomes turbulent. One side of the ball is spinning in the same direction as air rushing by, and the other side of the ball spins against the wind. This causes a difference of air resistance between the two sides of the ball, and according to Bernoulli's principle, it will move in the direction of least pressure.

So when a right-handed pitcher throws a curve, he spins the ball clockwise and it curves to the right. Spinning it counterclockwise is a screwball, which curves to the left. If he gives the ball topspin it will sink, and backspin makes it rise (or, strictly speaking, it will not *drop* as much as it would under the force of gravity alone).

Dr. Lyman J. Briggs of the National Bureau of Standards has claimed that the maximum amount a baseball can curve is 17.5 inches, and the most effective speed for the nastiest curveball is 68 MPH. The more rotation, the more curve.

Oddly, the *less* rotation the pitcher puts on the ball, the more it curves also. A knuckleball is thrown with little or no spin by keeping the wrist stiff and pushing the ball off the fingertips (not the knuckles). The pitch, invented by Larry Cheney in 1912, flutters to the plate at about 65 MPH and is notoriously hard to hit, catch, or umpire. "It looks like a pigeon coming out of a barn door," says Bob Feller.

When asked how he handled the knuckleball, former catcher and celebrity beer drinker Bob Uecker says he would pick it up after it stopped rolling. As far as hitting it goes, Charlie Lau once said, ''There are two theories on hitting the knuckleball. Unfortunately, neither of them works.''

It was once believed that knuckleballs behaved erratically because they were buffeted to and fro by puffs of wind (which, if true, would make the pitch useless in every domed stadium). In 1975, Tulane engineers Robert Watts and Eric Sawyer published ''Aerodynamics of a Knuckleball'' in *The American Journal of Physics,* which proved that it is the raised *stitches* on the baseball that cause the knuckleball's unpredictable wiggle.

Watts and Sawyer put a baseball in a wind tunnel and noted that the stitches disrupted the flow of air around the ball, creating an asymmetrical wake and pushing the ball this way and that. The ball, in effect, runs into a wall of air. This air piles up on the stitches and pulls the ball in the other direction.

The best knuckleball is one that rotates slowly. As the changing orientation of the stitches bumps into the airflow, the ball may curve more than once on its way to the plate.

''Were the ball to become smooth, knuckleball pitchers would disappear from the major leagues overnight,'' claims physicist Cliff Frolich of the Institute for Geophysics at the University of Texas.

And if the Haitian women who hand-sew major league baseballs decided to raise the seams a fraction of an inch, they would give a tremendous advantage to knuckleball pitchers. For many years the baseballs used in the American League and National League were sewn together by different companies, with the National League balls having higher seams. It was probably not entirely coincidental that the National League became known for breaking-ball pitchers while the American was dominated by fastballers.

Far from behaving erratically, the knuckleball actually follows the laws of motion to the letter. If a pitcher were able to throw the pitch exactly the same way every time, holding it in different stitch orientations, he could predict its trajectory and actually spot the ball. Dr. Joel Hollenberg of New York's Cooper Union recently updated Watts and Sawyer's knuckleball research with a computer simulation that does just that.

According to Hollenberg's computer, if the pitcher holds the ball at a tilt angle on the longitudinal axis of -15 percent, a release angle of 3 degrees, and throws a 70 MPH knuckleball that spins 10 degrees per second, the ball will cross the plate 2.81 feet above the ground and .42 foot to the first-base side. That is, if the temperature outside is 75 degrees Fahrenheit and the barometric pressure is 14.696. Perhaps someday pitchers will come to the mound armed with a load of computer printouts.

The reason the knuckleball is so tough to hit is that it does most of its movement *after* the batter has started his swing. Every Little Leaguer has been told: "Keep your eye on the ball!" but recent research shows that to be impossible. University of Arizona engineer Terry Bahill measured eye and head movements and found that even the quickest batters lose sight of the pitch once the ball is 5.5 feet from the plate. At that point, the ball is moving three times faster than the eye can track. The human eye simply can't see the ball hit the bat.

"Maybe the human eye doesn't, but mine does," says Keith Hernandez.

In any case, Bahill has actually suggested batters take their eyes *off* the ball in the middle of its trajectory and shift their field of vision closer to the plate.

The batter has to plan his swing and guess where the pitch will wind up after seeing just the beginning of the ball's trajectory, so if a pitcher can make the ball change course at the *end* of its flight, the pitch is virtually unhittable. That's exactly what a good knuckleball does.

"If you can throw a pitch that exhibits its most erratic motion in the last two-thirds of its trajectory, the batter will have a very difficult time," says Joel Hollenberg, who became intrigued with fooling batters while sitting in a 75-cent bleacher seat watching Don Larsen's perfect game in the 1956 World Series.

A good knuckleball may be unhittable, but the fact that there are only four or five knuckleballers in the major leagues suggests how difficult it is to throw the pitch consistently. To solve this problem, pitchers have come up with *other*, more devious means of making a baseball dance after the batter has begun his swing.

The Right Scuff

Scuffing the ball causes an aerodynamic effect similar to that produced for a knuckleball by raised stitches. If the surface of the ball is made irregular, the airflow around it becomes turbulent. This turbulent air causes the wake to move toward the smooth side of the ball. Air resistance is increased on the side of the ball that has been altered and it will veer the other way. The rougher the surface, the more the ball will veer off course.

When Dodger pitcher Jay Howell was nabbed with pine tar in his glove during the 1988 playoffs, he claimed it improved his grip but did not affect the flight of the ball. However, the last time anybody looked, Jay Howell did not have a degree in physics. If it improved his grip, the pine tar made it possible for Howell to put more spin on the ball, which certainly affected its flight. Just about anything you do to a sphere will make it deviate from its basic path, and pine tar is a foreign substance.

Because the ball already has raised seams, Dr. Joel Hollenberg believes tampering with the ball is unnecessary. ''To me, the whole idea of roughing the ball up is absurd,'' he says. ''It's just like training wheels on a bicycle. A pitcher who understands how to use the roughness of the stitches doesn't have to do anything to the ball.''

Ballplayers, however, believe cutting or scuffing the surface of the ball has more of an effect than the stitches do by themselves. According to catcher Gary Carter, ''An illegal pitch moves in so many different directions, many more directions than a good knuckleball.''

This could be because unlike a knuckleball, a scuffball is thrown hard and spins. You can't spin a knuckler because the stitches wrap all around the ball and would effectively cancel each other out. A scuff, on the other hand, can be placed in one spot and the ball spun around that spot.

It's also possible to make one side of the ball rougher than the other by making the other side *smoother*. In the 1982 World Series, Bruce Sutter was observed rubbing the ball briskly against his uniform in order to throw a ''shiner,'' which is also illegal.

Ted Williams says in his autobiography that ''pitchers as a breed are dumb and hardheaded,'' but it cannot be denied that they are also quite resourceful.

The Search for the "Dry Spitter"

The recent success of the scuffball has taken the classic spitball off the front pages, at least for the time being. Spitballs, like knuckleballs, have little spin. The wrist is held stiff and the ball is squirted out of the fingers, something like shooting a watermelon seed. A good spitter looks like a knuckleball and dives as it approaches the plate.

The old explanation for the physics of the spitter was that the weight of the saliva somehow tipped the ball over. Actually, the slippery substance on the fingertips reduces the friction that normally comes with throwing an object. Instead of spinning backward as it leaves the hand, the ball will have no spin, or a slight topspin. It doesn't really matter what foreign substance is put on the ball, but pitchers have tried anything they can sneak out of the dugout.

○

After doctored pitches were banned in 1920, pitchers and pitching coaches began searching for deliveries that could mimic the action of the spitball legally—a "dry spitter." The knuckleball served this purpose, as it does today, but it was difficult to throw.

The slider was invented by George Blaeholder of the St. Louis Browns in the late twenties and eventually became popular as "the Pitch of the Sixties." It looks like a fastball, but just as the hitter reacts, the ball breaks down and across. It's thrown something like a football. When the pitcher releases it, he gives a little twist, sort of like turning a doorknob.

The split-finger fastball ("the Pitch of the Eighties") has been popularized by Roger Craig, but was invented by Bert Hall back in 1908. In those days it was called a forkball. Both pitches are thrown today. The forkball is held deeper in the hand with the fingers spread apart and is used as an off-speed pitch, while the split-finger is thrown harder, like a fastball. Hitters say it drops like a rock.

Because of all these "dry spitters," it is getting harder and harder to identify an honestly illegal pitch. "There was a time years ago when a guy would throw a spitball and it would react totally differently than his other pitches," says sixteen-year American League umpire Joe Brinkman. "But because of the split-finger fastball and other new pitches where the bottom drops out, you can hardly tell any difference."

As is usual with dry spitters, there is talk that the split-finger fastball is so effective and easy to throw that it's making illegal pitches obsolete. But in time hitters will figure out how to hit it and somebody will come up with *another* dry spitter. In the meantime, cheating goes on as usual.

Nice Day for Cheating

Baseball cheaters should take their craft seriously, as even atmospheric conditions will have an effect on their efforts. A ball that is hit will travel as much as twenty feet farther on a hot day, in high altitude, and in humid air because there is less drag, according to Dr. Robert Watts of Tulane University. A scuffer or spitballer will get better movement on the ball in cool, dry air, especially at low altitudes. The ball won't break as much in Mexico City (7,350 feet above sea level) as it will in Yankee Stadium (55 feet). If they ever award a franchise to Death Valley (282 feet below sea level), it would be prudent to strip-search all pitchers between innings.

Knuckleballs and spitballs are more effective against the wind than with it, and in high barometric pressure than in low. "It's when you get a wind blowing in behind you that you fear," says king of the knuckleballers Hoyt Wilhelm. "A knuckler seldom does anything then, because it's a nonrotation pitch that does better against air resistance."

If managers were smart, they would start their curveball specialists on days when the air is cold and heavy, and fastballers when it is hot and dry.

How are managers, coaches, and players using all this valuable scientific information? Hardly at all.

"Baseball players basically are stupid and the people who run the game are stupid," complains Pete Brancazio. "It's an extremely tradition-bound, anti-technological game. When they're looking for young pitchers, they take the radar gun and if a kid can throw 85 or 90 MPH, that's what they want. If there's a pitcher with a great curveball who can mix his pitches up, they're not interested. They want people who can throw hard."

When asked if he has a scientific theory on why there was suddenly a barrage of home runs a few years back, Brancazio responds, "Yeah. Lousy pitching."

If it appears that pitchers have more illegal weapons at their disposal, batters may get some consolation from the fact that a doctored baseball travels *farther* when hit than a legal ball. The irregular surface breaks the symmetry of the airflow around the ball and causes aerodynamic lift, the same way dimples make a golf ball sail. That is, of course, if the batter can manage to get a piece of the doctored ball in the first place.

It probably all evens out in the end. The pitchers have their sandpaper, the batters their cork. The more the pitcher scuffs the ball, the farther it will fly when the batter gets hold of a fat one. So the perfect balance between batter and pitcher—which makes the game of baseball so fascinating—is preserved, even among cheaters and scoundrels.

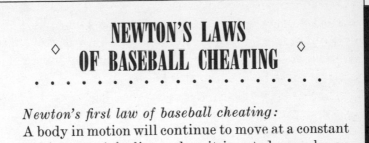

NEWTON'S LAWS OF BASEBALL CHEATING

Newton's first law of baseball cheating:
A body in motion will continue to move at a constant speed in a straight line unless it is acted upon by an unbalanced force.

Yeah, like Vaseline.

Newton's second law of baseball cheating:
A body will be accelerated when acted upon by an unbalanced force.

Yeah, like a corked bat.

Newton's third law of baseball cheating:
For every action there is an equal and opposite reaction.

Yeah, and if you get caught corking a bat or scuffing a ball, you'll be suspended for ten days.

The "phantom double play." The second baseman gets the force even though he's nowhere near the bag. Notice that the runner (Billy Martin) doesn't even slide toward the base, but toward the fielder instead. (*National Baseball Library, Cooperstown, N.Y.*)

Umpire Red Jones ejected fourteen members of the Chicago White Sox when they jockeyed him during a game in 1946. (*Associated Press/Wide World Photos*)

Leo "Screechy" Durocher, the king of bench jockeying. Note the bats in front of the dugout. Bat racks were around in 1948, but Leo liked to watch opposing catchers try for foul pops on a bed of rolling lumber. (*National Baseball Library, Cooperstown, N.Y.*)

Ted Kluszewski hit the long ball by banging nails into the surface of his bats. He also intimidated opponents by cutting off the sleeves of his uniform shirt, as shown here. (*National Baseball Library, Cooperstown, N.Y.*)

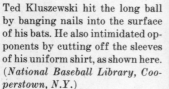

The lost art of "bat boning." Players used to harden their bats by rubbing them over a hambone. Joe DiMaggio demonstrates proper boning form. (*National Baseball Library, Cooperstown, N.Y.*)

Hall of Famer Burleigh Grimes threw the last legal spitball fourteen years after the pitch was outlawed. (*National Baseball Library, Cooperstown, N.Y.*)

Three-foot, seven-inch Eddie Gaedel walked on four pitches in a 1951 game. The next day it was ruled that midgets couldn't play professional baseball. (*Associated Press/Wide World Photos*)

Johnny Bench with a "cupped" bat. Perfectly legal, and physicists say hollowing out the end is just as effective as illegally filling a bat with cork. (*National Baseball Library, Cooperstown, N.Y.*)

The already classic George Brett "Pine-Tar Episode." (*National Baseball Library, Cooperstown, N.Y.*)

It wasn't until after Sam Rice died, in 1965, that he revealed what actually happened in the 1925 World Series. (*National Baseball Library, Cooperstown, N.Y.*)

LEFT: Mike "King" Kelly. On one occasion, he was sitting in the dugout when an opposing batter hit a pop foul. "Kelly now catching for Boston!" he yelled, and grabbed the ball. This prompted a rule change prohibiting substitutions in the middle of a play. (*National Baseball Library, Cooperstown, N.Y.*)

RIGHT: Doctoring baseballs was legal in the Negro leagues. "Smokey Joe" Williams, seen here, was a master of the emery ball. He won the "Battle of the Butchered Balls" against Chet Brewer in 1930, striking out twenty-seven in twelve innings. (*National Baseball Library, Cooperstown, N.Y.*)

Connie Mack brought his gentleman's touch to the rowdy world of baseball in the early days. (*National Baseball Library, Cooperstown, N.Y.*)

7th
INNING

The Morality of Cheating:

Would Jesus Throw a Spitter?

"I'd trip my mother. I'll help her up, brush her off, tell her I'm sorry. But Mother don't make it to third."

—Leo Durocher

You'll notice that this is one of the shorter chapters. That's not to say there's no morality in baseball. There's just very *little* of it. If there were a whole lot of morality in baseball, you wouldn't be reading this book.

But professional athletes do face tough questions regarding right and wrong. If there were a version of the board game of *Scruples* for major league baseball players, it might have a question like: *Your teammate and best friend scuffs the ball in a secret way that only you know about. If he were traded to another team and threw a scuffball to you, would you tell the umpire how he did it?*

A player who cheats must figure out not only how to get away with it, but also how to live with himself when the game is over.

Early in the 1978 season, someone approached Cleveland's slugging first baseman Andre Thornton and gave him an illegal cork-filled bat. Thornton used it and hit one home run with it (off Mike Torrez of the Boston Red Sox). But the experience made him feel so guilty that he discarded the bat and switched back to a legal one two weeks later.

"It gave me a tremendous emotional problem," Thornton said. "I used a dark bat and no one ever would have known. But I couldn't find peace with that, even though a lot of players use them. I just couldn't use something illegal and live with myself. I felt so much joy when I discarded that bat, you can't imagine.

"All men face such decisions, in any walk of life. Do you cheat? Or do you rise above it?"

Rising Above It

For most players the answer is easy—you cheat. But occasionally—*very* occasionally—someone will rise above it. San Diego

Padres pitcher Eric Show has been known to ask umpires to remove scuffed balls when he comes across them. "If I can't get the hitters out legitimately," says Show, "I don't want any part of this game."

Al Worthington, who pitched for the Giants in 1959, was asked to use binoculars to steal signs from opponents. He refused, saying he would not play for a team that cheated. San Francisco obligingly traded Worthington to Boston, perhaps a more law-abiding environment. No dice. Boston traded him to Chicago, who traded him to Cincinnati, who traded him to Minnesota. Four teams in four years. It must be tough to find a town that welcomes a guy with a conscience that's better than his curveball.

"Worthington's ethics are wonderful for a game between the Humane Society and the Salvation Army," said Rogers Hornsby. "But not in the majors."

Guilt is not completely absent from the major league personality. After Rick Honeycutt was nabbed on the mound in 1982 with the thumbtack sticking through a Band-Aid, he said, "I wanted to tell everybody that I was really sorry, that what I did was stupid and that I'd never do it again. I never wanted this to happen, and I didn't know the consequences."

That's a rare exception. Most players caught cheating seem to have failed to grasp the idea that they have done anything wrong. Joe Niekro's only regret over his much publicized sandpaper incident was that he never received any offers to do endorsements from companies that make power tools.

For most players, like most of us ordinary people, the only thing that prevents them from disobeying the rules is the most primitive form of morality—the prospect of getting caught. Pete Rose once revealed that he had used an illegal bat in practice, but wouldn't dare bring it into a game. Not that he was against the idea on moral grounds. "I always thought that if I got caught," Rose explained, "every one of those damn hits I got, people would think I cheated."

Unfortunately, Rose's reputation got tripped up in other ways.

Baseball's Mixed Messages

Baseball walks a tightrope when it comes to right and wrong, cheating or playing by the rules. On one hand, here is a game that is heavily based on deceit and deception. As we have seen in previous chapters, it lends itself very well to an almost un-limited spectrum of rule bending. The players, often poorly educated and rarely introspective, are competing for enormous sums of money, prestige, the adoration of fans, the thrill of winning, and a place in history. The general public will forgive them for cheating much more quickly than they will for losing. If they can't perform, there are a hundred guys dying to take their place.

It's the perfect atmosphere to encourage breaking the rules.

But then there's the other side of the coin. The structure of the game itself is almost ridiculously fair. A pitcher's perfor-mance is judged not by wins and losses, but by earned-run average, a statistic which carefully lays blame only on those who are responsible for failure. The infield-fly rule protects the runner from a situation that would be beyond his control. A hitter can advance the team cause by sacrificing his turn at bat to move a runner up a base, allowing the next man to drive the run in and get the glory. Even the object of each turn at bat— to return home—indicates a desire for order. George Carlin does a wonderful routine demonstrating that baseball is a warm and fuzzy sport, while football is hateful and mean-spirited.

Furthermore, our society values the trait of sportsmanship, and even the greenest rookie quickly learns how to play this game. "We respect the hell out of them. They played a great Series," he'll say, instead of what he may really be thinking— "We beat those bastards, and I hope they feel as miserable now as I feel happy."

Former baseball commissioner Ford Frick once said, "Base-ball never posed as a self-appointed leader in social and eco-nomic reform. It does not attempt to set legal precedents or standards of human behavior. In its sins and its virtues it only reflects the spirit of the times, a cross section of contemporary life.''

But because baseball so carefully merchandises its players as role models for the youth of America, they are expected to behave on a higher moral plane than businessmen, garbagemen, or members of any other profession. The game prides itself on being the National Pastime, and is very careful to protect its positive image.

Do Baseball Officials Encourage Cheating?

In ancient Greece, cheaters in the Olympics were disqualified, humiliated, and sometimes whipped in public. The Greeks apparently felt this punishment fit the crime. In baseball it's a good question: *Does* the penalty fit the crime? The usual penalty for cheating is a ten-day vacation and a fine of a few hundred dollars.

It can easily be argued that the men who run the game are *encouraging* cheating by the way they handle infractions. When Dodger pitcher Jay Howell was caught with pine tar in his glove during the 1988 National League Playoffs, there was such an outcry about the ''severity'' of his three-game suspension that Bart Giamatti, then National League president, reduced it to two days.

''The penalties being enforced now are a joke,'' complains St. Louis superstar Ozzie Smith. He points out that suspending a starting pitcher for ten days in the regular season may amount to his missing one game. If scuffing the ball will help that pitcher win twenty games and earn a million dollars a year, it simply makes economic sense to cheat. ''The fine has to be so severe that players won't want to risk getting caught,'' Smith says.

But if nobody gets caught anyway, it doesn't matter *what* the penalty is. Umpires are often criticized for not being more vigilant in catching cheaters. But can you blame them? In 1978,

Don Sutton was caught with a scuffed ball and ejected from a game by umpire Doug Harvey. When Sutton threatened to sue, the National League backed off and didn't penalize him. When umpires ruled that George Brett's infamous pine-tar bat was illegal and that the home run didn't count, the American League president overturned the decision and gave the home run back.

"We were overruled by our own league president," umpire Joe Brinkman said of the pine-tar incident. "We were demoralized by the president's decision." Understandably, umpires feel humiliated in these instances and are reluctant to stick their necks out to catch other cheaters.

"The umpires have admitted to me that they would do more if they felt the league was behind them," catcher Gary Carter said during the rash of cheating incidents in 1987.

"In my entire minor and major league career I never caught a single pitcher doing anything illegal," wrote former ump Ron Luciano in his book, *Remembrance of Swings Past.* "I didn't want to catch a pitcher for two reasons: one, the American League didn't want me to, and two, the American League *really* didn't want me to."

Why not? Wouldn't ridding the game of cheaters improve baseball? Well, not necessarily.

The commissioner of baseball is in a constant predicament. He would genuinely like to eliminate cheating, but catching cheaters is an embarrassment to the game and a humiliation for the players caught. What if Mike Schmidt had used an illegal bat? The man may someday be grouped in the same class as Mickey Mantle and Willie Mays. What umpire, league president, or baseball commissioner would want to taint Schmidt's reputation for life? The aging pitchers who were suspected of throwing scuffballs, including Tommy John, Joe Niekro, and Don Sutton, are future candidates for Cooperstown also, and baseball would prefer that they get inducted honorably.

The fact is, if baseball went after cheaters aggressively, they would have to throw out half the members of the Hall of Fame.

Furthermore, the commissioner knows that fans want to see their heroes play the game, not get kicked out of it. According to *Baseball by the Rules*, Commissioner Bowie Kuhn specifically instructed umpires *not* to eject manager Dick Williams or Blue Moon Odom in the 1972 World Series. The reason for this unusual ruling, the authors believe, was that millions of TV viewers would have turned off their sets if the game's star attractions were sitting around the clubhouse.

There is no doubt that baseball could put an end to cheating *immediately* by making it easier for umpires to catch cheaters, backing them up on controversial ejections, and instituting strict penalties. Oddly but logically, those actions could possibly hurt the game more than help it.

For these reasons, it's easy to understand why baseball encourages cheating, and why it doles out halfhearted punishments when forced to catch rule-benders in the act. The muddle of mixed messages has set up a twisted morality. The game has strict and clearly written rules, but they are not enforced and in some cases are almost completely ignored. Except for blatant offenses that cannot be overlooked, cheating is tolerated, and is actually considered to be just another skill, like hitting to the opposite field. To declare that the spitball, for instance, is illegal and then catch just two men throwing it in seventy years teaches no other lesson except that it's legal to do things that are illegal. Cheating is a part of the game.

There is no shame brought upon convicted cheaters. On the contrary, they are respected as clever competitors who do all they can to help their teams win. What does it say to the kids of America when Whitey Ford is inducted into the Baseball Hall of Fame after having written "Confessions of a Gunkball Artist"?

This lackadaisical attitude toward cheating has infuriated some people. In 1973, Bobby Murcer called Commissioner Bowie Kuhn "gutless" for not enforcing the rule against spitballs, specifically Gaylord Perry's spitballs. The same year, Texas Ranger manager Billy Martin ordered his pitchers to throw spitters in a game against Perry to demonstrate the mockery that was being done to the rule book. Rather than doing anything to stop Perry from throwing his spitter, baseball officials fined Murcer $250, Texas pitcher Jim Merritt $1,000, and suspended Martin for three days.

In other words, cheating is okay—but bringing it to anyone's attention is illegal.

How to Cheat and Still Sleep at Night

In the end, it's the players who have to do the actual cheating, and the ones who have to deal with the right and wrong of it. Assuming that all men have a conscience and feel a certain amount of guilt when committing an act they know is wrong, the question becomes: How can a man cheat and still feel good about himself?

Very rarely will a player look into the cameras or microphones and say, "I cheated and I know it's wrong. I have no apologies." That would mean not only committing a wrongful act but also showing no remorse for it. Instead, the player will always add a qualifier. "I cheated, but so does everybody else." "I cheated, but I didn't know that what I did was illegal." "I cheated, but my manager told me to."

Psychologists call these excuses rationalizations—defense mechanisms that preserve a person's self-esteem by creating a plausible explanation for unacceptable conduct. With a good rationalization that he can believe, a player can carry on cheating without confronting his conscience or values. He can still feel good about himself.

The most common rationalization is simple denial: "I didn't cheat." The player attempts to convince the umpires, fans, and himself that he is innocent of the charge. Despite the fact that umpires have confiscated overwhelming evidence of dozens of baseballs scuffed in exactly the same place, none of the accused scuffball pitchers has ever admitted (at least not in public) to any wrongdoing. Most accused cheaters simply deny everything, and it's hard to prove them wrong.

Players who have been caught or have admitted cheating must come up with more creative rationalizations to explain their behavior. These are a few of the most popular ones:

"I cheated, but the rules are unfair."
"I admit I broke a rule," Jay Howell said after getting nabbed with pine tar in his glove during the 1988 playoffs. "But I don't think it's a good rule." In Howell's mind, it's unfair to rule that using a sticky substance to get a better grip on the ball is illegal, so it's okay for him to break that rule. "I'm aware that it's illegal," Howell said. "But my intent was not to cheat."

"I cheated, but it wasn't my fault."
When his bat split open and Super Balls bounced out, Graig Nettles claimed that the bat had been given to him by a fan. Similarly, Houston's Billy Hatcher, when cork flew out of his bat, explained that he borrowed the bat from another player. We'll never know if these two gentlemen were telling the truth, but in their minds the crimes were not so severe because they didn't do the actual cork jobs themselves.

"The other guys get all the breaks, so it's okay for me to cheat."
Nearly all rule changes in baseball have favored the hitters. The ball has been juiced up, trick pitches banned, the mound lowered, fences moved in, and the strike zone tightened. These changes have become necessary because the art of pitching has advanced more than hitting has, and it would completely dominate the game if changes were not made.

Conveniently, pitchers can justify cheating by claiming they are being persecuted. "Everything is for the batter," com-

plained admitted spitballer Preacher Roe. "The rules makers
are against you." Gaylord Perry, king of the spitballers, once
whined, "The hitters are given every advantage, so we need
every trick we can get."

Hitters then turn this logic around to justify their own cheating. "I don't begrudge the pitchers," Graig Nettles said when
he played for the Yankees. "But until the umpires have the
guts to stop them from marking the ball, I see nothing wrong
with using a corked bat."

If everybody is cheating, *nobody* has to take the responsibility for breaking the rules.

"I cheated to put food on the table for my family."
Listening to pitchers talk, it sounds like they would all be
homeless if you took away their spitballs. "There comes a time
in a man's life when he must decide what's important," Gaylord Perry once said dramatically. "He must provide the best
way he can for his family. Hitters are taking the bread out of
your mouth. You have to learn all the tricks and then use them
when you have to."

That's a heartwarming message, until you consider the fact
that by cheating, Perry took more bread out of hitters' mouths
than the other way around.

Enough money and creature comforts can usually override
any ethical problems a man might have with cheating. Preacher
Roe once estimated that his spitball earned him $100,000. "I
have a nice home, a cabin just across the Arkansas border, a
small boathouse and I bought a good grocery business. Not bad
for a little ol' country boy," Roe said thankfully. "I'm for
spitballs. I like 'em."

During the scuffball scandals of 1987, somebody asked
Whitey Ford what he thought about cheating and Ford replied,
"If it were me and I needed to cheat to be able to throw the
good stuff that would keep me in the major leagues at a salary
of about $800,000 a year, I'd do whatever I had to do."

Of course, Whitey was throwing spitters, scuffers, and mud-balls when he was making $75,000.

"I only cheat when I need a big out."
A man can convince himself that it's acceptable to break the rules once in a while if he is honest the rest of the time. That makes it easy in baseball, when there are so many nonpressure situations. It would be pointless to cheat when you're pitching to a .198 batter with a big lead. You wait until the bases are loaded and the score tied to whip out an emery board.

I was watching a game on TV last season when I heard broadcaster Jim Palmer say of Gaylord Perry, "I admire him. He only cheated when he had to."

"I cheated to help my team."
Baseball and politics are two arenas where lawlessness is considered just if it serves a higher cause. When pitcher Kevin Gross was caught scuffing in 1987 and the Philadelphia Phillies chose not to pay his salary while he was suspended, Gross was outraged. After all, he had cheated for the sake of his team. "I thought my own team would have backed me," Gross said, "unless they don't give a bleep about me or my career."

"I cheated because I'm a competitor."
Cheating somehow has become equated with having fire in the belly. Real men cheat. Men who play by the rules are wimps. Nice guys finish last, as Leo Durocher once remarked, presumably because they don't have the guts to do what they need to do to win.

"Any pitcher who doesn't seriously consider an 'extra' pitch," manager George Bamberger once said, "you got to wonder if he really wants to win."

"That's not cheating, it's gamesmanship."
"Although scuffing and corking are called cheating, I really don't agree with the term," ex-pitcher Jim Kaat wrote in a

Popular Mechanics article on the subject. "I don't believe that taking an edge is cheating in the moral sense. Ballplayers call it gamesmanship."

Semantics is a handy way to make the best of a bad situation. When a euphemism is substituted for the cold reality of the word "cheating," it doesn't seem like such a bad thing. A cheater may toss and turn in his bed all night, but a man who practices gamesmanship can get a good night's sleep.

Another psychological term for this phenomenon is "cognitive dissonance." If you can't change your behavior, you change your *feelings* about your behavior and feel better about it. If you can't quit smoking, for instance, you convince yourself smoking isn't that harmful, so you won't feel so guilty about it. If you can't get anybody out without scuffing the ball, you convince yourself, for example, that the rules are unfair to pitchers.

Separation of Church and Dugout

The recent rise of religion in the clubhouse has made the morality—or lack of it—in baseball even more confusing. In the late seventies, Detroit sportswriter Watson Spoelstra started "Baseball Chapel," an organization that made it possible for teams to attend prayer services before games on Sunday. The idea has spread, and most teams now have a chapter. Many players in the game have become religious, and many count themselves as "born-again Christians." For a time the San Francisco Giants were referred to as "the God Squad."

While it's heartening to see that professional baseball players have deeper concerns than spotting cute girls in the bleachers, there is nothing to suggest that the increase of religion in the clubhouse has cut down on the amount of cheating on the field. One can't help but wonder how a deeply religious player can attend a prayer service in the morning and throw a scuffball that afternoon.

Not all observers believe religion and baseball mix. A few years ago there was an outcry when Bob Knepper, then with the San Francisco Giants, gave up a game-winning home run and told reporters it was ''God's will.'' Knepper denied the quote, but there has been some concern about the intensity of the ''born-again'' players. When one believes that everything is in God's hands, success as well as failure can be easily explained without taking blame personally. The religious player might well wonder why he should play the game with all the intensity he can muster when a higher authority has determined who's going to win.

Ex-catcher and broadcaster Tim McCarver says, ''In my opinion, baseball 'chapel' doesn't belong in a baseball locker room any more than a pepper game belongs in the aisles of a church.''

During a tight game in 1977, Baltimore outfielder and born-again Christian Pat Kelly was up with the bases loaded and a full count. Kelly took a wild swing and struck out on a pitch that would have surely forced in the run. The next day, after the team's chapel service, he bumped into his manager, Earl Weaver.

''Skip,'' asked Kelly, ''don't you want to walk with the Lord?''

''I'd rather you walk with the bases loaded,'' Weaver deadpanned.

A few days later, the persistent Kelly pushed his luck and asked Weaver when was the last time he got down on his knees and prayed.

Weaver replied, ''The last time I sent you up to pinch-hit.''

◇ THEY SAID IT ◇

• • • • • • • • • • • • • • • • • • •

"Christ might not throw a spitball but he would play hard within the rules."

—*Fritz Peterson*

"If God let you hit a home run the last time up, then who struck you out the time before that?"

—*Sparky Anderson*

"The game is in a sorry state if success is based on willful violation of the rules."

—The Sporting News

"Conscience? Hell, it never bothered me none throwing a spitter."

—*Preacher Roe*

"The great American game of baseball is a fraud, a treachery and un-American. It offers a regrettable example to the nation's youth, is populated by cheats, thrives on sneaky tricks, and teaches Fagin values to thousands of Little Leaguers. It is corruptive and should be repressed. And as sometimes played by major leaguers, it is . . . fascinating."

—*Shirley Povich,* Washington Post *columnist*

"Baseball fits America so well because . . . it expresses our longing for the rule of the law while licensing our resentment of law givers."

—*A. Bartlett Giamatti, former baseball commissioner*

• • •

◇ THEY SAID IT ◇

• • • • • • • • • • • • • • • • •

"The rules of baseball were written exceedingly well, but they were written *by* gentlemen *for* gentlemen. They should have been written for professional athletes who were, in the main, completely unfamiliar with the meaning of the word 'gentlemen.' "
—*Bill Klem, Hall of Fame umpire*

"Baseball is not, nor does it profess to be, a builder of human character or a champion of moral uplift. It is a game—and a good one!"
—*Ford Frick, former baseball commissioner*

"If you're a pro, then you often don't decide whether to cheat based on if it's 'right or wrong': you base it on whether you can get away with it."
—*George Bamberger*

"The 'anything to win' spirit which has made the Cleveland ball park a travesty on good sportsmanship is the same fundamental corruption that is eating at every part of the moral fiber of American life."
—Christian Century, *commenting on the groundskeeping tactics of the Cleveland Indians*

"A guy who cheats in a friendly game of cards is a cheater. A pro who throws a spitball to support his family is a competitor."
—*George Bamberger*

• • •

◇ **THEY SAID IT** ◇

• • • • • • • • • • • • • • • • •

"Pitchers have been cheating for many years and only periodically have the umpires made a serious effort to catch the offenders. I feel that was because they so rarely received backing from the league offices to really go after the rule breakers. In my view the league offices simply relaxed the rules and allowed pitchers to get away with cheating."

—*Frank Robinson*

• • •

7th

INNING

STRETCH

Chatting About Cheating

Bowie Kuhn, Former Baseball Commissioner

Q: Tell me about the time you caught Charlie Finley cheating.

This has got to be the 1973 Series. It was beginning to get sort of dark. In the bottom half of the inning—and this game was being played at Oakland—Charlie had the lights turned on. He obviously did it at that time to advantage his team, which was at bat. They would see better. Under World Series rules, you can't turn on the lights during the game without the consent of the umpires. That is designed to prevent any team from advantaging itself by turning on the lights whenever it suits their purpose. So Charlie went ahead and turned on the lights when it suited his purpose, and he got fined. You just don't do that.

Q: As commissioner, what was your attitude toward teams and players who cheated?

I've always been uneasy with those aspects of the game where teams try to cheat on the rules. Sometimes there's a nice distinction, but in many instances it's perfectly, transparently cheating. You set a good example for an easily impressed public that follows you, and you are doing a public service. I felt baseball should be a public service in that sense. It should try and set some kind of example that would be good for kids. Cheating on the rules suggests to kids who follow baseball with a loving affection that it's okay. So it's very simple with me—that kind of stuff bothers me.

There's a nicer area of gamesmanship that doesn't bother me. The White Sox, if I recall, were famous for damping down the field because their runners didn't run as fast as some other teams. That's an old baseball trick. It doesn't bother me. If that's a bad thing, we can pass rules saying how you can or can't water the field. But we've always tolerated that, so I think that is a kind of permissible gamesmanship.

Q: But as a fan, wasn't it a little titillating when an emery board flew out of Niekro's pants a few years ago?

I think it's lousy. Plain and simple.

Q: Do you at all admire a guy who cheats, for his desire to win?

I would never fail to distinguish the two thoughts. As lousy as I think flagrant cheating is, I certainly can stand off in another direction and admire the will to win of our athletes. Nothing appalls me as much as an athlete who makes a half-effort. I admire the spirit and the will to win and the will to be as good as you can be. I just deplore the fact that it sometimes slips into cheating.

Q: Umpires, and Ron Luciano in particular, have complained that they don't catch more cheaters because they aren't backed up by league officials.

I think Luciano is wrong on his basic theory. I think the umpires are backed up and I think the league presidents certainly did want to catch cheaters. I'm not saying there may not have been a time fifty years ago when it might have been different. I don't know. But certainly in the time I was commissioner and the time I've been around baseball, I don't think there was any desire to avoid catching cheaters. I think they've always wanted to catch cheaters.

Mookie Wilson, Toronto Blue Jays

Q: When somebody is cheating against you, do you complain?

Why complain? Hey, what are you going to do? How are you going to prove it? Because all you know is what you think. You say, "I think it was an illegal pitch." What's the umpire going to do? "You *think* it was an illegal pitch?" I have them check the ball all the time, but I have them check it for dirt clogs or something that might make it move. I don't have them check it for no scuffs. I would never do that. Ever.

Q: So you just don't concern yourself with pitchers cheating?

I don't worry about it. I cannot hit worrying about what the pitcher is doing. That's why I don't even concern myself with it. So if someone is throwing me scuffers or spitters or something, more power to 'em. He still has to have some kind of control. You can't worry about that stuff. It's too tough hitting as it is.

Q: In 1986, the media said Mike Scott was doing exactly that—making the Mets worry too much about cheating.

That's possible. And half the time he wasn't doing a thing. Maybe he didn't do anything. Maybe he did. But it served the purpose. Because if you're thinking about something other than hitting, he doesn't *have* to do anything. Or any other pitcher, for that matter. I've seen balls with scratches on them. To me, I just can't see how that makes a big difference. Somebody who knows what they're looking for would probably notice it more. When you hit like I do, you don't worry about those things.

Q: Have you ever been tempted to use a corked bat?

I don't really believe in corked bats. You gotta make contact. What good is a corked bat if you're gonna pop up balls anyway? You gotta hit the ball solid. I don't see what difference it's going to make, to be honest with you.

Q: When a pitch is coming in, can you tell if it's illegal?

No. Not really

Q: There's not a big difference between a good sinker and a spitball?

Yeah. But you wouldn't know it until after the fact. You can tell the difference between a spitter and a good sinker. The movement of the ball. The rotation of the ball. That's the difference. The spitter don't rotate. You know if a sinker sinks abnormally for the guy that you're facing. That's about all you can say. You can suspect that something is different, but you really don't know. Anyone who says, "I know every time somebody throws a funny pitch"—you can't possibly know every time. It's impossible. You just can't.

Dave Winfield, New York Yankees

It's all part of sport. Everybody's always looking for an edge in this game. It's just that the public never knows about it. You know? Does a guy take pills before a game to play? Does a guy get drugged? Does a guy get shocked? Who knows? Some guys might use an oversized glove, but so what? They'll do anything. It's a game, it's a sport, it's a science, it's a business.

Q: How do you hit an illegal pitch?

The same as you hit a legal one. But you don't go up there determining if it's legal or illegal or even think about it, because you're going to strike out.

Q: Do you know one when you see one?

Sometimes. After they throw it. But it's too late then anyway. They can't take it back. They're going to do it, just like guys are going to cork bats and hit home runs.

Q: Is a real good scuffball hittable?

Of course.

Q: Have you hit them?

Of course. But they can't throw them all the time. They can't get up there and scuff, cut, or put soap or tar on the ball every pitch. And even if they could, they couldn't get it over every time. And even if they could get it over, they'd hurt their arm.

Q: Did guys always cheat as much as they do now, or has the big money added motivation?

It's to hang around. It's to put up as good numbers as you can and hang around.

Q: So a guy at the end of his career will be looking for that edge more than a guy who's just breaking in?

Or a guy with no velocity or no confidence in his pitches.

Q: What about hitters?

I don't know. I've never had to cheat. I get 'em with what I've got.

Bill James, Author and Sabermetrician

Q: Have you looked at statistics of guys who played both before and after the spitball was banned to see how it affected their careers?

Sure. This is not just an era where there were a lot of great hitters, but an era in which the circumstances were favorable to hitters. If you look at hitters who were twenty-seven years old in 1918, what you'll find is that they were better hitters five years *later* than they were in their prime. That's extraordinary. That's not true of any other generation of players.

Q: What would Wade Boggs hit if trick pitches were legal today?

Oh gosh. The people who have thrown the spitball have said it is extremely difficult to master, and that makes sense to me. They tell us that just a little drop of moisture will make a ball act funny if you know how to deal with it. I think it's probably as difficult to master as any other pitch. If you went back to the "emery ball" days,* the league would lose thirty points. But just legalizing the spitball would have a very dramatic effect on a very small number of pitchers—the few who can master it. And that might cause batting averages to drop ten points or so.

Q: When guys get caught cheating or admit cheating, should we take their statistics with a grain of salt?

Well, I'm not a terribly moral person, but I tend to think about rules in terms of *effective* rules. If a rule is not being enforced, if it's not being called, in effect it doesn't exist. If you try to make it exist, you get into all kinds of absurdities. There's no doubt that Steve Carlton committed two thousand balks in his career if the balk rule was enforced by its current standards, but how can you make an adjustment? How can you make his stats into what they would have been if they called a balk on him every time he didn't come to a stop?

* "Emery ball" was an early moniker for a pitch made with a defaced ball.

Gaylord Perry's teams won ballgames that they would have lost otherwise and maybe even won a pennant that they would have lost otherwise. I don't think you can adjust those wins out of existence. If they couldn't enforce the rule when he was on the field right in front of them, there's no way they can enforce it now.

Brooks Robinson, Hall of Famer

I used a corked bat in an Old-Timers' home-run-hitting contest in Denver about five years ago, and I won the contest. I was fixin' to go up to hit and Jose Cardenal said, "Here, use this bat. I've corked it." And I really believe I hit the ball further using that bat. From my experience, I think the ball does go further.

I remember we were playing against Nettles one time. He swung and the whole bat just exploded. All this cork rolled out the end of it and everything. They threw the bat out of the game, of course.

I can't remember anyone on our club corking a bat. I think you would probably know who was doing something like that. I used to see Russ Snyder boning his bat almost until it was flattened out on one side, you know. It wasn't illegal, and I guess he was trying to compress the wood and make a flatter hitting surface. But he'd take one swing and break it after boning it for a month!

Q: What was Earl Weaver's attitude toward cheating?

Weaver always had the philosophy that he had the best players, so he didn't want to get into any knockdown contests and he felt the same way about players doing things illegally. I'm sure we've had guys throw spitters—Ross Grimsley loaded them up now and then—and you didn't say anything about it.

Q: Did Grimsley feel guilty about throwing a spitter?

No, I don't think so. He resorted to it late in his career. I mean, nine out of ten of these guys, if you ask them if they throw a spitter, they're gonna say no. Even now, it would probably be tougher to detect than ever before because a lot of pitchers are throwing the forkball that reacts the same way. But the guys are not going to admit to it.

Q: Did Grimsley admit it in the clubhouse to his own teammates?

No, not really. It was just common knowledge and when someone would say something, you'll get a little sly smile out of him. I'll tell you, the spitter is used more as a psychological ploy than anything else. When you know somebody's got an extra pitch and you don't know when he's gonna throw it, in the back of your mind you've got to say to yourself, "This guy throws a spitter." Your concentration suffers more than anything else. Some guys take pine tar and moisten it. You get a very slippery effect. That can act as a substance for a spitter and you don't have to go to your mouth to get it.

The thing about the spitter is that not that many guys threw it. Number one, they couldn't control it. You don't want to use it on every pitch. You use it as an element of surprise. You get to a situation where a guy has got the bases loaded and two strikes on the hitter. You're trying for a strikeout more than anything else. That's when you drop a spitter in. When you throw it every pitch, it's really not that effective.

Gaylord Perry could psych guys out because they knew he threw it. But he might not throw it more than once every two or three hitters. He went through all these preliminary deviations and things just to kind of set you up for the one you were gonna get. That's why you don't have more guys throwing it. Some guys can't throw it, some guys can't control it.

Q: Did you see a lot of scuffing when you were playing?

We went through a big rigamarole with Jim Bunning. We thought he was scuffing them up. When you continuously get balls that are thrown out of the game that have big gash marks on them, you say to yourself, "Somebody's doing this. Is it the catcher or is it the pitcher?" We swore it was Jim Bunning doing it. I mean, these were real gash marks. They thought he was doing it with his belt buckle when he would bring the ball across his belt. But nothing was ever proven. I mean, how ya gonna prove that?

Q: You're a religious man. How does a deeply Christian ballplayer handle the question of whether or not to cheat?

That's a good question. I would think that the guys who were religious probably would not cheat. I would think they would have a hard time rationalizing something like that. But it's a game of survival a lot of times, and that takes over more than anything else. I mean, if you're in the major leagues, and you're on your way out, and the only way you can get by is by throwing a spitter, then you would really have to sit down and think about it if you were a really religious guy.

Earl Weaver, Former Manager

You remember the Phantom Pickoff? It was the greatest play that was ever invented. The pitcher's on the mound with a man on first. He steps off. Now he can fake a throw to first. All in one motion, he fakes a throw to first and the runner dives back. The first baseman dives over the runner going back. There's no ball, but they're faking like the throw went down the right-field line. The ballgirls in the bullpen are in on the act, yelling "Here it is, here it is!" The runner takes off for second. The pitcher has the ball in his hand, turns around and throws it to the shortstop, who tags him out.

I saw it pulled in the College World Series. Nobody knew where the ball came from. Even the first-base umpire went running down the right-field line trying to find the ball. If I'd have known about it, I would have tried that play in the major leagues. That play is 100 percent legal.

Q: In the 1969 Series, you disputed a play when Cleon Jones of the Mets was hit on the foot and Gil Hodges proved it by showing the umpires the ball with a black smudge mark on it. Did you think Hodges put the shoe polish on the ball?

I have no idea. Whether he put the shoe polish on it or not nobody will ever know. But my contention was that once the ball went into the dugout, there was no way the umpire could tell how the shoe polish got on there. Once you lost sight of the ball, let's don't use that as any criteria as to whether it hit Cleon Jones or not.

Q: You've said the spitball is an overrated pitch.

There's gonna be a lot of them that don't do anything. And it's a tough pitch to master and control. I think if it was legalized, the hitters would learn to lay off it more. It goes straight down and out of the strike zone frequently. I don't think it does any more than a split-finger fastball. The motion on the ball is the same. It's something that the hitters don't get to see on every at-bat, which really makes it the effective thing. You don't figure it's in a pitcher's repertoire. It's easier to throw a bad spitter than it is to throw a bad split-finger fastball.

Q: Why don't you think Mike Scott has been caught scuffing?

I don't think he's cheating. I think he's just got an outstanding split-finger fastball. He learned how to use it and he learned how to use it effectively. That's it.

Q: Now that you're retired, any complaints about baseball?

Probably the stupidest thing since I got out of the game is that a manager can go out and have one bat confiscated per game. I'll tell you what it does. It takes the umpire right off the hook, which is silly. Once he does that, eight guys can come up there with corked bats and he can't say a thing. The umpires are intelligent enough to see if a bat's been tampered with. The confiscated-bat rule ought to be out and just give it to the umpires.

Q: How did you feel about pitchers on your team cheating?

Well, you call it cheating.

Q: Call it throwing a spitball . . .

Which is illegal. Rather than cheating, doing something illegal. I've had pitchers use the spitball. How do I feel about it? My conscience? I'm not going to be in favor of anything illegal. I wasn't happy with it, but I certainly wasn't going to take a weapon away from somebody who was trying to help us win games. What you're doing is turning your head. Whether that's right or that's wrong is a tough question. When somebody employed something illegal against us, I made my protest.

Q: Would that include one of your players who was traded?

Oh, definitely. Yes, if I could. I'd say, "Listen, this guy pitched for me. I know what he's doing. Now watch for it." The umpire's in a terrible spot. He'd say, "Earl, if I see anything that looks strange, I'll do something."

Umpires have warned pitchers. That's their job. They don't like to do it. But it's got to be enforced. There were some umpires who would say, "Get out of here, I'm not going to do a thing about it and if you come out here again you're out of the game." It's as simple as that. Now your hands are tied. That kind of an umpire should be reported and was reported to the American League president. And something should have been done.

Q: You say it would bother your conscience when players cheated. Did the players themselves ever feel guilt?

They're trying to make a living to send their children through college. They're going to use anything available. As long as it's not harmful to another human being.

Q: But what about the *other* guy's children?

Roger Clemens can throw the ball ninety-eight miles an hour. He's trying to take a living away from Cal Ripken, Jr. Okay, what are they gonna do, make him throw the ball eighty-five miles an hour? No. That's the object.

Q: But Clemens is getting guys out with his own skill.

And so is the other guy.

Bill Robinson, New York Mets Coach

Q: You once got into a brawl with Rick Rhoden over illegal pitches. How do you handle them when opposing pitchers throw them?

If I see it, I do something about it. I have my own way of doing things, my own conscience, and I can't speak for anyone else.

Q : Are there more illegal bats now than when you were playing?

Nobody really thought about corked bats much when I was playing. I don't know if there was as much, or more, but nobody ever really said anything about it. I really don't think a lot of guys did it. If they did it, it wasn't really brought to anyone's attention.

Q : Is baseball more tuned in to cheating now?

Both the National League and American League presidents are dealing with the integrity of the game more now. That's their job. They've really cracked down on the balk rule and that's changed the pitchers a little bit.

Q : What about the umpires? Do they police the game adequately?

The umpires have a thankless job. I really sympathize with them. They get it from one side or the other. They can never make anybody happy. I think they put a clamp on it. They control the game. Some umpiring crews control the game a little more than others. But they let you know right off the bat that they're not going to stand for this or that.

Don Zimmer, Chicago Cubs Manager

I don't see why everybody doesn't just have an X-ray room in every ballpark. If they think people are corking bats, let the umpire run in and shoot an X ray. If it's a legal bat, let the guy hit with it. Why should somebody think I hit an illegal home run?

The only time I ever saw a corked bat was when I watched Billy Hatcher in 1987. We were in San Francisco when he hit the ball and his bat broke in half and there was the cork. That's the first time I ever saw it. Now that doesn't mean that I never looked at a corked bat, that I wouldn't know it. I never seen anyone cork a bat, and I've been in the game forty years.

There must be something to a corked bat that makes the ball go further. Otherwise they'd let it be legal. When you see little guys hitting home runs to the opposite field, something's going on. Maybe that had something to do with all the home runs last year. When they clamped down with the X rays and so on, the home runs disappeared.

Q: Do you think they should bring back the spitter?

They made the spitball illegal for a reason.

Q: Since then, a lot of people have argued in favor of legalization.

Who's a lot of people? Pitchers?

Q: Ford Frick, Casey Stengel, Joe Cronin...

I never heard that. There's a reason it's illegal. I mean, somebody could get hurt. Sometimes you don't know where the ball is going when you throw a spitball.

Q: Couldn't the same be said of a knuckleball?

Yeah, but a knuckleball ain't illegal.

Harry Caray, Chicago Cubs Announcer

I don't see any reason why the spitball shouldn't be legalized. It doesn't do any more than a knuckleball or a split-finger fastball. You know how traditional baseball people are. The important thing is, to make a lousy goddamn buck the commissioner of baseball forces the Cubs to put in lights with the threat that if they're in the playoffs or the World Series, without lights, they'll transfer the games to St. Louis. Is that a crock of shit?

Richie Ashburn, Hall of Famer

When I played on the Chicago Cubs, we stole signals from the centerfield scoreboard. It was a white dot out there that they'd cover on one pitch. It was very easy to pick up. And I've played against teams that have had people in the centerfield stands with binoculars stealing catcher's signs. I was taking 'em, along with everybody else. It helped. You always have a better chance when you know what's coming.

But the recent bat thing surprised me. I never even thought of anyone corking a bat. And I'm not even sure that corking a bat helps. The hitter might mentally think he has an edge, but I don't think they do much.

I remember Del Ennis used to soak his bats in oil. He'd stick a couple of dozen in a barrel of oil at the end of the season and soak them there until the next year. It permeates the structure of the wood. I used to take a nail and groove out the soft part of the grain. Then, as you use the bat, it fills in with dirt or whatever and it makes the hitting surface harder. But I never really considered that cheating.

Q: What was your impression when Kevin Gross of the Phillies was caught cheating a few years ago? (Ashburn is a Phillies broadcaster.)

I knew about it. He really wasn't trying to keep it a secret. Let me put it this way—it was an open secret on the ballclub that he had this sandpaper. But when I discovered it, I was surprised that Kevin did it because he didn't need to. He had a good enough arm and good enough pitches where he didn't have to do anything illegal. Oddly enough, he was hit a lot harder while he was pitching illegal than when he was legal.

Everybody says Don Sutton does this to the ball and Mike Scott does this. I think pitchers look around and see this guy who was just a mediocre pitcher until he came up with the split-finger fastball. Well, a lot of people think it was a split-finger, some people think it was a doctored ball. Then they say, "By golly, *I'm* going to try that. Maybe *I* won't be mediocre anymore." But Kevin got caught and he's been a better pitcher since.

Q: In your playing days, the spitball was more popular than the scuffball.

I played against spitball pitchers. Lew Burdette was one. Preacher Roe, Gaylord Perry. Perry had a tremendous fastball and sinker. I don't think he really needed to cheat. I know Don Drysdale, late in his career, cheated with a spitter. Stan Williams too. Maybe it was because they thought they were losing something and they wanted to get a little more movement on the ball. Gaylord Perry was an outstanding pitcher. Would he have been otherwise? I don't know. Maybe *he* doesn't know.

Q: If Billy Hatcher had won the batting crown the year he was caught cheating, do you feel it would be right to let him keep it?

Well, they only caught him once. I have a tendency to think he should keep it had he won the batting title. Because I don't care what you got in that bat, you still have to make good contact. If he'd have hit sixty-five home runs and knocked in a hundred and fifty runs with that bat, then I'd say let's kind of put a disclaimer on those records.

Tom Heitz, Head Librarian, National Baseball Hall of Fame

Q: What types of cheating went on in the early days of the game?

There's a fine line between strategy and cheating. In the Massachusetts style of the game, there was no foul territory, and sometimes batters would follow the pitch through and hit it in the opposite direction of the pitcher. This was called back-hitting. They would place three or four catchers behind the batter.

Bunting was unknown then. It would have been very effective, but it would have been frowned upon as lacking pluck. ''Pluck'' is the nineteenth-century word for ''macho.'' Someone who bunted was seen as doing something unmanly, effeminate. Dickie Pearce, a shortstop from the 1870s, was generally credited with popularizing the bunt. Pearce evidently overcame any scruples he had or others had with that being improper, and it became a regular part of his strategy and later copied by others.

Many baseball innovations—stealing bases is another example—were at one time not considered cheating, but at least unsportsmanlike and ungentlemanly. There was an unwritten code of fairness among gentlemen, and sliding into a base feet first or diving into a base would have been regarded as ungentlemanly conduct in the Massachusetts game. The game was played on one's feet. One did not grovel in the dirt and soil his clothes.

By the Civil War period, the emphasis was on playing the game hard and playing to win and we were beginning to desert that concept of a gentleman's game. Some of these things we take for granted now, really began as strategy and some might have regarded that as cheating. But in the absence of a rule covering such things, it was hard to characterize it as cheating.

When those things begin to occur, you're faced with the question of whether you need a rule or not. And those who made the rules decided at one point or another that they were going to outlaw certain things and accommodate others. Bunting was not outlawed, so the perception was that it was a viable and useful part of the game and a useful strategy to employ. So there are certain things that we say serve no useful purpose or are beyond the veil of decency in the game and may lead to injury.

In town ball, they had "plugging" or "soaking" the runner—putting the runner out by hitting him with the ball. The New York Knickerbockers found that distasteful and undignified. A man might get hit in his private parts or in the face. So they did away with that and instituted the force play and the tag in place of plugging. Plugging was one of the most exciting plays. They had no basepaths and the runners would run all over the field to avoid being plugged. Now we take the force play and tag for granted.

In many cases, the rules are not an attempt to shape the game, but simply to react to something that has happened in the technology of the game or in the way the game was played. For instance, there were no pitching mounds when pitching was done underhand. An underhand thrower has an advantage from a flat surface or throwing from a slight depression. In 1884, overhand throwing became allowed for the first time and the overhanded thrower has a slight advantage throwing from a slight incline.

Nobody knows exactly how the mound came into being. The first mention of the mound in the rule books is in 1904, when the elevation was limited to fifteen inches. That's twenty years after overhand pitching was allowed. In baseball, the response sometimes comes years after the fact.

The invention of the glove is another thing. Originally, gloves were protective devices, not catching devices. When they became catching devices, rules had to be imposed or the gloves would have grown and grown. People would be stealing home runs and outfielders would have these huge things on their hands.

Q: Couldn't it be argued that corking a bat adds another enhancement to the game, the same as the pitching mound and the glove, and the same way fiberglass revolutionized pole vaulting and tennis players now use oversize rackets?

Well you have to decide just what technology you're going to incorporate into the game. If that decision is made consciously by all concerned, then I don't think it poses a problem. People have talked about electronic foul lines and laser-controlled strike zones and all this sort of thing. We have to recognize that someday we may incorporate these things into the game.

Astroturf is an interesting example. We've had Astroturf for more than twenty years and statistically I think everyone is satisfied that playing on Astroturf lends a different complexion to the game. The ball bounces differently. There tend to be more infield hits. This is a good example of a situation where baseball has tolerated differences. There's a lack of uniformity because not all stadiums have artificial turf. There are economic and political factors that have outweighed uniformity in the game.

Q: What were the factors surrounding the banning of the spitball in 1920?

It was outlawed following a public health crisis which rose to the character of the present AIDS scare—influenza, cholera, and tuberculosis. Influenza was not a well-understood disease. It decimated thousands, if not millions of people during World War I. We had sanitariums that were loaded with people suffering from these diseases and they could be spread through contact with saliva. The knuckleball and curveball were no more or less effective than the spitball, but it was the perception that spitting on the ball was unsanitary that led to the outlawing of that pitch.

Q: Do you consider cheating to be part of the game's folklore?

I come from a legal background and have a law degree, so maybe my answer is colored a bit. There are degrees of things in this area. I don't know that some of the tampering done rises to the character of a felony, let's say. Its appreciable effect on a competitive edge is negligible. The advantage may be more in the mind of the player perpetrating the events than it is in reality. It may be a little bit like jaywalking. Something people do every day and don't get tickets for. It's the sort of offense that we tolerate up until a certain point, but if somebody abuses it too much we give them a ticket. There are certain types of behavior in baseball, as in life, that we contemplate are going to happen. There may be instances where they get away with it. If they're caught, we punish them, but not severely. And there is a class of offenses in baseball of that sort.

Q: Was there ever any discussion about booting Whitey Ford or other players who admitted to having cheated out of the Hall of Fame?

In my mind, it diminishes the respect we have for such players to some degree because it demonstrates the disregard on their part for the rules of baseball and for competing on a fair and equitable level. I don't know that Whitey's using thumb-tacks really was that much benefit to him. He clearly seemed to think it did at the time.

Howard Cosell, Television and Radio Broadcaster

Q: What is your impression of all the corking and scuffing episodes that have been taking place recently?

Oh God, that's for children. Who cares about that? You're writing a book about cheating in baseball, which I consider the most narrow, unimportant topic in the entire world. I don't see you writing about a legal monopoly—cheating in the National Football League, where hundreds of people have been check-ered in one way or another. I don't see you writing about the violence and the mess in ice hockey. I don't see you writing about the whole of sports. You're writing about Gaylord Perry! I've dedicated my life to justice and honesty in sports and to the absence of racism in sports and to the things that matter in sports. Not about Gaylord Perry in the Hall of Fame, which as a matter of fact, I would vote him in, having just had Gabe Paul as a guest for a week at my house. And he said, "That man was a great pitcher. Of course he belongs in the Hall of Fame." So what? I mean, I don't believe you. Look at profes-sional boxing if you want to deal with cheating and immorality. Sports are chewing up this country. They're destroying it. And that's the broad picture of sports, which thoughtful people know. But good Lord, cheating in baseball? The real problem is the warped values that people place on sports. Where are the values? Cheating in baseball has never been symptomatic of the society. Cheating in sports is symptomatic. Crookedness and corruption in sports is symptomatic of the society.

Q: You were a fan of the Brooklyn Dodgers when you were

growing up. Did it bother you when Preacher Roe admitted he threw a spitter the entire time he was with Brooklyn?

It was a matter of total insignificance to me. I didn't care. It's not important to a man like me. It's obviously of super importance to a man like you. The only thing significant to me about the Brooklyn Dodgers was because of Jackie Robinson. They had a place in the American history books.

Q: If you feel that this topic is so insignificant, why did you do a TV show training cameras on Gaylord Perry to find out if he was throwing a spitball?

For the fun of it.

Q: Do you feel people are basically dishonest and only play by the rules because they're afraid of getting caught?

Oh my God. Start reading. Go back to Thoreau. Read Kant.

Don Mattingly, New York Yankees

Q: Do you think corked bats work?

Oh, I'm sure they work. I would think they work. I mean, you put cork in there it's just like anything else. Like an aluminum bat. I've tried cupped bats, but I don't like the balance. I like a solid piece. Basically, you order your bats a certain weight. If they're cupped, they give you a heavier piece of wood, take the weight out and you still have 32 ounces. That's what I always use, even at the end of the season. I wouldn't want to use a corked bat.

Q: Would you be able to tell the difference between a split-finger fastball and a spitter?

I'd be able to see the difference. I've just never really seen them.

Q: What about scuffballs?

I don't know anybody who scuffs it. I don't think I've ever faced anyone who scuffs the ball. I don't know if I've seen one or not.

Q: If you did see it, how would you go about hitting it?

I guess it would be instinct. It would be something like hitting a sinker. A guy that makes the ball run, it would be the same thing.

Q: Do you look for a sinker?

I want the ball to be up. If a guy sinks it, I might have faced a guy like that and just thought he was sinking it, and just try to make him get the ball waist-high.

Q: Does a sinker do the same as a split-finger?

No. Different pitches altogether. The split-finger dives. The sinker runs and down, and the split-finger looks like a fastball and goes straight down. A split-finger looks more like a fastball, until the end.

Q: Do you do anything to psych out pitchers?

The only way to psych out a pitcher it to hit him hard every time. In some guys you see fear, I think a lot. They pitch scared. Like they don't have confidence in themselves. But I don't think about it too much when I'm out there. Just kind of see it and hit it and leave it at that.

Gary Carter, New York Mets

Q: In 1986, you and the Mets were pretty vocal about Mike Scott, claiming he scuffed the ball. Looking back, do you think he psyched you guys out?

I guess you could say it was psyching out a little bit. But nonetheless it's one of those things that you just go with the flow. There's not a whole lot you can do about it. As a result, we ended up winning the Series, so that's the most important thing. I'm just kind of grateful we didn't have to face Scott in game seven.

Q: When all that was happening, why didn't you just cheat back? Couldn't Dwight Gooden throw a dynamite scuff if he wanted to?

Maybe, but I just don't think he had practiced with it, so he may not have had the same kind of control. That's the way you look at it. It's not an eye for an eye, a tooth for a tooth. That's not the way we play this game as far as I'm concerned. I guess maybe what we should have done was cork all our bats then. No, he got away with it, and you've got to tip your hat to him, I guess. I mean, it was pretty obvious what he was doing.

Q: There don't seem to be as many complaints about Scott anymore.

Maybe he's watching what he's doing now. I don't think he's doing it quite as much. I think the league is watching it a little more, too.

Q: Do you admire him as a pitcher?

Do I need to answer that?

Q: It's up to you.

I'd rather not.

Q: When a guy is cheating, do you admire him for his will to win, or is he making a mockery of the game?

No, I don't think he's making a mockery of the game. But I do believe that there are a lot of pitchers who will do things to keep themselves in the game. Now, at one point in time of Mike Scott's career, he was only mediocre at best. There was even a chance that the Astros were going to let him go. Then he turns into a great pitcher. I guess you can give him a salute for being able to come up with the split-finger, which was what he says is what turned him around. But I think the sandpaper helped him a lot too. But, you know, pitchers can do that and I know quite a few pitchers who have done that to have their careers continue. And they'll keep doing it until they get caught or they just can't get anybody out with it anymore. That's the way this game goes.

Bob Feller, Hall of Famer

Q: Does a guy who cheats admit it to his teammates?

It's obvious to a guy's teammates when somebody is cheating. Even a corked bat. It's kind of hard to hide those things around the clubhouse. I've known fellas to do this on my own ballclub.

I won't name names. Sometimes they'd flatten the bat down or peel it down or shave it off or put wire brads in there. It didn't make all that much difference.

Tampering with the ball is different. I saw guys put mud in the seams. If you get a ball that's been hit real hard off the wall, it may be scuffed or it won't be completely round. So when you pitch that ball, it's going to move. Normally, a pitcher will never throw a ball out of the game voluntarily if he thinks he can use it to his advantage.

Q: Did it bother you at all that guys on your team were doing illegal things?

It didn't make us feel good about guys who cheated. You figure they cheat at the ballpark, they'll cheat on the golf course, they'll cheat in business, and anything else in life. Players may laugh about it and say it's funny, but right down in their heart, they don't think it's funny at all, and they have no respect for a person who cheats. I don't think any manager is going to tell a pitcher who's winning not to be doing something to the ball. But I'm sure that down in their heart they have a different feeling than what they would professionally.

Q: Why do you think guys cheat?

Usually people cheat in sports because of a lack of ability. The best players don't have to break the rules. But a lot of the fellas who cheat, they could get by with their own natural ability. Some people in life would cheat to make a dollar, but if they were honest and worked harder, they could make ten dollars. Same thing in baseball. Perfect your skills if you have 'em and if you don't have 'em you shouldn't be playing. The rules are there. If you can't live and win within the rules or within the law, that's not what this game is all about or what life is all about. If you can't live within the rules, you should be penalized according to whatever the penalty may be.

Q: So who's at fault for all the cheating that goes on?

I blame the umpires more than anybody else. If I were an umpire and saw a pitch coming up there that looked like it had been tinkered with, I would take the ball immediately and look at it. If it was roughed up or fluffed up, I would throw him out of the ballgame the first time and give him a good, stiff fine. Maybe the next time I would give him a little rest for thirty days. Enough is enough. You can stop it right there at the plate. I could never figure out why they don't do that.

Q: Was there as much cheating in your playing days as there is today?

Long before my day, there was more going on. Say back before World War I. The balls weren't as good. The conditions weren't as good. Supervision wasn't that good. Nowadays with television and replays, everybody's watching everybody else. They don't get away with anything.

Q: I guess you didn't need to cheat, because you could throw the ball ninety miles an hour.

Yeah, and that was my change-up.

Mel Stottlemyre, New York Mets Pitching Coach

I don't think I'm getting in trouble by saying that if my guys get a scuffed ball that someone else has used and left in the game, they know what to do with it. I'm not teaching them how to scuff it. I have taught some guys what to do if a ball has a scuff on it. I don't think there's anything damaging in that.

Q: So which opposing pitchers leave the most scuffed balls lying around?

I think in one case I know Mike Scott has been accused of scuffing the ball a great deal. I'm not flat-out accusing him, but I know that in one game Ron Darling pitched against him, he got a lot of balls that had scuffs on them and I think we used them to our advantage. It's hard to accuse a guy unless you catch him barehanded, but I know that in some games we had against Rick Rhoden when he was with Pittsburgh, our guys felt he was doing a lot of things to the baseball that they reacted funny.

Q: Do you do anything about it?

I don't make a big issue out of it. I collected the balls for a while because we were getting a lot of them. I check them occasionally if I see a pitcher throws a few funny pitches that don't react normally. There's not much you can do about it. They can be sent to the league president and all that, but nothing is really done. I suppose there's no way of completely getting rid of it. I think they watched Scott real closely for a while and they tried the best they could to catch him. I guess the bottom line is they still have to throw it across the plate, throw it for strikes.

Lance Parrish, Catcher, California Angels

You know, it's difficult to say somebody is cheating now because guys throw that split-finger fastball. It's got an unnatural movement to it. It's more difficult for the umpires to prove a guy's doing anything or not now unless they catch a guy with something on him.

I'm not an expert on scuffed balls, but I know that if you take a scuff and throw it the right way, it will move for you. I've played catch with guys who have taken a scuffed ball and said, "Okay, I'm gonna make it do this." And then they do it. I've seen it work. If you work on it you can control it, if you know what you're doing. The thing about it is, if you use a ball for an inning and the ball bounces in the dirt or hits something, it's going to scuff. But unless you know what you're doing with it, it's useless.

Stephen Ciacciarelli, Editor, *Baseball Illustrated*

You hate to think of guys using corked bats, and I think a lot of guys are unjustly accused. I hate to make a general statement, but I think pitchers are much more guilty than the hitters. It's always gone on. Now they seem to be scrutinizing it a little more carefully. I think if baseball used replays the way football does, it would make it much harder to cheat.

I think right now the increased vigilance is bad for the game, but in the long run it's going to be good. What it's going to do is make the players' awareness of these rules much clearer. Players are going to abide by the rules more closely and get in the habit. I think in the long term there will be less cheating and it will be a much more honest game.

From a professional standpoint, I lose respect for a guy who cheats. But from a fan's standpoint, I say the guy's got gumption. From the fan's view, if you can pull it off, great. The main objective is to get on base and cross home plate no matter how you do it.

Robert Godfrey, National Baseball Fan Association

I feel that tampering with bats is much more serious than scuffing balls. With one swing of the bat, those guys can determine the outcome of a game. When a pennant race is decided by a game or a half a game, that's a big difference. A scuffed ball, there's not as much of a control factor on it. The guy's not exactly sure what the ball's going to do. A batter can take a pitch. He's got more than one shot at it. So I don't think the advantage is nearly as much in the pitcher's favor with a scuffed ball as it is in the batter's favor with a corked bat.

Q: Would you like to see the spitball legalized again?

It's still a ball that you're throwing. It might move a little bit differently, but they didn't ban the knuckleball. Spitballs and greaseballs and everything else have been around ever since the start of the game pretty much. I don't have a big problem with them. Guys still hit their home runs.

Q: If you were the commissioner, how would you punish cheaters?

If I were the commissioner of baseball, I'd nail them to the cross. I think cheating is wrong. I'd have suspensions much greater than the ones that are issued today.

9th INNING

Great Moments

. . .

The Last Legal Spitball: September 20, 1934

The spitball was officially banned in 1920, but the last completely legal spitball wasn't thrown until fourteen years later. Of the sixteen pitchers who were permitted to keep throwing the pitch for the rest of their careers, Burleigh Grimes hung around the longest. Every spitter he threw was legal, so his last one was the last legal spitball.

Grimes took the minor mystery of that specific pitch to his grave with him in 1985, mostly because nobody ever bothered asking him exactly which pitch was the last spitter he threw until forty years later. Tom Heitz, head librarian at the Baseball Hall of Fame, popped the question when Burleigh was eighty-eight. Grimes simply couldn't remember.

The best guess is that he threw it in his last major league appearance, which took place on September 20, 1934. It was the end of a season in which Grimes, then forty-one, had already bounced from St. Louis to the Yankees to the Pittsburgh Pirates, and had won just four games. In the eighth inning of a losing cause against the Brooklyn Dodgers, he was called in to pitch. He retired the side in order, striking out one batter. The last hitter he faced was "Jersey Joe" Stripp, and because Grimes threw the spitter frequently, we can only presume that Stripp was on the receiving end of the last legal spitball. Grimes didn't get into any more games and he retired, taking the spitball with him.

Others, of course, carried on the tradition.

The Most Famous Spitball: October 5, 1941

The spitball is not only difficult to hit; it is also tough to *catch*. The most heartbreaking muff in baseball history was the spitter that Mickey Owen dropped in the fourth game of the 1941 World Series.

Let's set the classic scene: Ebbets Field. The Yankees are up, losing 4–3. Two outs in the ninth inning. Nobody on. Full count on Tommy Henrich. One lousy strike and the Brooklyn Dodgers will tie up the Series at two games apiece.

"With the count 3–2 on Henrich I figured I'd throw him a curve and put everything I had on the pitch," Dodger pitcher Hugh Casey told reporters at the time. In later years, Casey admitted that what he meant by "everything I had" was that he threw Henrich a spitball.

Casey got the one strike he needed. Henrich ("Old Reliable") swung and missed, the game so obviously over that security police began to run on the field. The only problem was that the ball squirted away from catcher Owen and rolled all the way back to the Dodger bench. By the time Owen ran it down, Henrich was at first. The Yankees were still alive. It truly ain't over till it's over.

As fate would have it, Joe DiMaggio stepped up and lined a single to left. Then Charlie Keller doubled in both runs. The Yanks stormed back and took the game 7–4. Instead of a tie Series at two games each, it was instantly 3–1. One Dodger fan listening on the radio was so frustrated by the incident that he threw his dog out an apartment window. The next day, the Yankees put the demoralized Dodgers away for good. It would be the first of six years that the Yankees would beat the Dodgers in the World Series.

Half a century later, people still remember the Mickey Owen muff. Hugh Casey passed away in 1951, but both Owen and Henrich claim the pitch was a curveball, not a spitball. "Spitballs drop down. I swung at a big breaking curveball," Henrich told sportswriter Dave Anderson. "It was a curveball," recalls Owen. "That's what I called for. But if Casey threw a spitball, he threw it on his own."

That may have been the problem. If Casey had let his catcher know the spitter was coming, Owen would have caught the ball and would not have had to go through the rest of his life known as the guy who blew the World Series.

Gaylord Perry's First Spitball: May 31, 1964

If you had been at Shea Stadium on this day, you would have witnessed more than a doubleheader between the San Francisco Giants and the New York Mets. You would have seen thirty-two innings—ten hours—of baseball. You would have seen forty-seven strikeouts, thirty-seven hits in one game, one triple play, Willie Mays playing shortstop, and Orlando Cepeda stealing home.

And you would have seen twenty-five-year-old Gaylord Perry throw his first spitball in a major league game.

Perry was a struggling relief pitcher at the time (2–1; 4.77 E.R.A.). "I was the 11th man on an 11 man pitching staff," he recalled in his book, *Me and the Spitter.* "The 12th man was in Tacoma." In the second game of the doubleheader, after the Giants had used up all their *good* pitchers, Perry got the call in the thirteenth inning. The score was tied at 6–6.

He got through the thirteenth and fourteenth innings with his fastball and curve, but in the fifteenth Jim Hickman led off with a single and was sacrificed to second. Perry's battery-mate Tom Haller jogged out to the mound.

"Gaylord," he said, "it's time to try it out."

Perry had learned to throw a spitball back in his North Carolina youth from a local hero named Skip Gardner, but he had never used it in a game. Now it was the moment of truth.

"I knew I was taking a chance on getting kicked right out of baseball for throwing the spitter," he recalled. "But it was either that or wearing out the seat of my britches on the bullpen bench till it was time to hang up my spikes and head home to the tobacco fields of North Carolina.

"I thought of my beautiful North Carolina wife, Blanche, our nineteen-month-old daughter, Amy, and our twenty-six-day-old, Beth. Mamma and Daddy back home on the farm. All counting on me."

You never thought the spitball could be so melodramatic, eh? Anyway, Mets catcher Chris Cannizzaro stepped up to the plate. Perry licked his fingers, pretended to wipe them off, and let loose that first hellacious spitter.

"She dropped into the dirt like a shot quail," Perry said.

It would be nice to say that Cannizzaro struck out on three straight spitballs, but trivia fanatics will remember that he walked. By the fifth pitch, Casey Stengel was already yelling "Spitter, spitter!" from the Mets dugout. The next batter, pitcher Galen Cisco, bounced a spitter back to Perry, and the Giants managed to toss the gloppy ball around for an inning-ending double play. Perry had the spitter working.

The Giants couldn't hit Cisco either, and the game stretched into the night. By the twentieth inning, Perry ran out of saliva and somebody gave him a slippery elm tablet to chew on. Finally, in the twenty-third inning, San Francisco pushed two runs across and won the game 8–6.

The mediocre young spitballer had pitched a remarkable ten shut-out innings in relief, struck out nine batters, and was credited with the victory. It was his seventh major league win, and he would have 307 more before hanging up the spitter nineteen years later.

The Great Potato Incident: August 31, 1987

It happened in a Double A game in Pennsylvania. The Reading Phillies had the winning run on third with two outs in the ninth. Williamsport catcher Dave Bresnahan told the umpire his glove was torn and ran back to the dugout to get a new one. He came out with another glove—and a freshly peeled potato.

After catching the next pitch, Bresnahan whipped the potato past third baseman Oscar Mejia and out into left field. Rick Lundblade, the runner on third, saw what he thought was an errant pickoff throw and scampered home. Bresnahan (the grandnephew of Hall of Fame catcher Roger Bresnahan) was standing there with the game ball in his hand and triumphantly tagged Lundblade out.

The old hidden-ball trick strikes again. When your team is twenty-seven games out of first place, you'll try anything.

Reading manager George Culver naturally protested and the umpires agreed with him, ruling that the run counted. Bresnahan was thrown out of the game, fined fifty dollars, and given his release. "It was an unthinkable act for a professional," said Williamsport manager Orlando Gomez. (It should probably be mentioned that Bresnahan was hitting .149 at the time and was on the way out, anyway. If he had been in the .300s, he would probably have gotten a bonus for his ingenuity.)

The story has a happy ending. The potato incident made Bresnahan a celebrity, in an odd sort of way. The story was all over the national news. At Williamsport's last home game, admission was reduced from $2.75 to $1 for any fans that brought potatoes to the ballpark. Bresnahan was on hand to autograph them.

A year later, Williamsport held a special day in honor of Bresnahan, who had retired from baseball to become a real-estate salesman. After his number had been painted on the fence at Bowman Field, he said, "Gehrig had to hit .340 and play in more than two thousand consecutive games to get his number retired. All I had to do is hit less than .150 and throw a potato."

The 1½-Inch Strike Zone: August 19, 1951

"I have examined the rules of organized ball and can't find a single paragraph which states how tall or how small a player must be to be eligible to play," said St. Louis Browns owner Bill Veeck. So, with his bizarre sense of humor, Veeck put a midget to bat in a major league game and it became one of the most memorable days in baseball history.

Previously, James Thurber had written a "short" story for the *Saturday Evening Post* in which a midget named Pearl DuMonville pinch-hit in the majors (he dribbled a 3–0 pitch to third and was thrown out). But Veeck claimed he had never read that story—he got the idea as a boy when John McGraw told his father, Bill Veeck, Sr. (president of the Chicago Cubs), ''We could have beaten you even with our batboy in the lineup.''

To make the stunt all the more outrageous, Veeck decided to unveil the midget at a fiftieth-anniversary party for the American League, with Baseball Commissioner Happy Chandler in attendance at Sportsman's Park in St. Louis. Between games of the Sunday doubleheader, jugglers and trampoline artists performed on the field, and Satchel Paige played drums. Few in the stands suspected anything historic when a giant papier mâché cake was rolled out to the pitcher's mound and Eddie Gaedel, a midget wearing a Browns uniform, popped out.

But they began to get the picture when the game started. Before the Browns' first batter came to the plate in the first inning, the public-address announcer informed the crowd, ''Batting for Frank Saucier, number one-eighth, Eddie Gaedel.''

Three-foot, seven-inch, sixty-five-pound Gaedel, a Chicago errand boy, strutted out of the dugout. His baggy uniform had been borrowed from nine-year-old Billy DeWitt, son of the Browns' vice president. Gaedel was swinging three little bats, just like a real major leaguer. Everyone in the ballpark was delighted, with the possible exception of Frank Saucier (who, with a career batting average of .071, could hardly complain about anybody pinch-hitting for him).

Umpire Ed Hurley, in charge of defending the dignity of baseball, called St. Louis manager Zack Taylor out of the dugout. Taylor was prepared, carrying Gaedel's official American League contract (it called for one hundred dollars for each game played) and other papers proving the midget had been added to the roster legally. Veeck had also taken the precaution of arranging insurance for Gaedel, in case of ''sudden death or sudden growth.'' Hurley had no choice but to carry on with the game.

Detroit left-hander Bob Cain, who found the whole situation

amusing, suddenly came to the realization that it was no joke
and that he'd have to pitch to Gaedel. He called catcher Bob
Swift out to the mound to talk strategy. Cain wanted to toss
the ball underhand, but that was illegal. Swift wanted to sit
on the ground to receive the pitches, but umpire Hurley
wouldn't hear of it. After fifteen minutes of discussion they
decided—logically enough—to pitch *low*.

Gaedel went into his batting crouch, leaving a strike zone
that Veeck had personally measured out at 1½ inches high.
Veeck had prepared Eddie, who had never played baseball
before, by giving him one simple batting tip: ''If you swing
at a pitch, I'll kill you.''

As the crowd giggled uncontrollably, Cain threw four balls
out of the strike zone, two of them way over Eddie's head.
Gaedel scampered to first, patted pinch runner Jim Delsing on
the rump, shook hands with the first-base coach, took a bow,
and marched off to history. Cain walked the next (regular-
sized) batter, too, but St. Louis wasn't able to score and eventually lost the game 6–2.

The next day, American League president Will Harridge
issued a statement condemning Veeck and the stunt. He declared Gaedel's contract to be illegal and quickly passed a rule
that all player contracts had to be approved by the league
president in advance. (Gaedel's ''statistics'' are listed in *The
Baseball Encyclopedia,* but every effort has been made to cut
his name out of the game's official records.)

Veeck, always ready with a quip, griped that Harridge's
decision was ''unfair to the little man.'' He went on to complain
that overly tall men like Ted Williams (6′ 3″) should not be
allowed to compete because they tend to hit home runs, while
Gaedel merely walked. Veeck actually had thoughts of replacing the pathetic Browns with an all-midget team, who would
happily take walk after walk and would be unbeatable.

According to Gerald Eskenazi's *Bill Veeck: A Baseball Legend,* Veeck wrote a letter to Harridge after the incident saying,

"Let's establish what is a midget in fact. Is it three feet six inches? Eddie's height? Is it four feet six? If it's five feet six, that's great. We can get rid of Rizzuto."

After it was all over, Eddie Gaedel became a local hero of sorts, even popping off in the press that he wanted to face Bob Feller next. He carved out a nice baseball career for himself. On one occasion, he was booked for a game in Chicago where he and three other midgets dressed as Martians "kidnapped" Nellie Fox and Luis Aparicio between innings.

Ten years after his moment of glory, Eddie Gaedel was mugged in Chicago, crawled home, and died. Only one baseball person showed up at the funeral—Bob Cain, who'd thrown him four straight balls out of the "strike zone."

The Forty-nine Year Putout: October 10, 1925

The story is told that Ken Berry, Chicago White Sox outfielder, once tumbled into the first row of the bleachers in an effort to snare a home-run ball. He didn't catch it, but Berry always carried an extra baseball in the back pocket of his uniform pants. When he hit the seats, Berry simply took out the extra ball, stuck it in his glove, and held it up for the umpire to see. Since the umpire hadn't leaped over the wall himself, he had no choice but to rule the play a legal catch.

There aren't many ways for outfielders to cheat and it doesn't happen that often. But the most intriguing instance took place in the 1925 World Series between the Washington Senators and the Pittsburgh Pirates in Griffith Stadium. The amazing thing is that it took forty-nine years to determine exactly what had happened.

Earl Smith, the Pirate catcher, hit a long drive to deep right centerfield. Sam Rice, a future Hall of Famer, leaped and caught up with the ball just as his body was hurtling over the fence. A full ten seconds passed before Rice got up, with the ball in his glove. Umpire Cy Rigleer called the batter out.

The Pirates argued that Rice hadn't caught the ball, that Washington fans in the first row had picked it up and stuck it in his glove. They went so far as to produce fans who witnessed the play and were willing to sign sworn statements that Rice had not caught the ball. Rice kept his mouth shut about what really happened, claiming, "The secret is more fun."

Over the years, however, the secret began to gnaw at Rice and he decided that it would be unfair to the baseball fans of the world if he were to pass away without revealing the truth. In 1965, he wrote a letter to the National Baseball Hall of Fame explaining his version of the play, with specific instructions that it not be opened until after his death. He died at the age of eighty-four in 1974 and the letter was finally opened.

This is what it said:

"I jumped as high as I could . . . and the ball hit the center pocket in the glove (I had a death grip on it) . . . at no time did I lose possession of the ball."

So finally, nearly half a century after the fact, Rice confirmed that he hadn't cheated. The catch had been ruled correctly.

Or so he said. . . .

The Pine-Tar Episode: July 24, 1983

The most famous baseball bat in the world isn't in Cooperstown. It's in a restaurant in Hermosa Beach, California. George Brett's restaurant. "Batgate," or "Tar Wars," as the incident is sometimes called, was a national sensation in the summer of 1983.

Sometime in the fifties, players started putting beeswax, elm resin, and pine tar on their bats. They're foreign substances, but are perfectly legal. Rule 1.10c clearly states: "The bat handle, for not more than 18 inches from its end, may be covered or treated with any material or substance to improve the grip. Any such material or substance, which extends past the 18-inch limitation, shall cause the bat to be removed from the game."

Brett, who always hit without batting gloves, slathered quite a bit of pine tar up the bat handle, and Yankee third baseman Graig Nettles spotted it one day.

''When we were playing the Royals in Kansas City, I noticed that George Brett had too much pine tar on his bat,'' recalled Nettles. He passed along the word to manager Billy Martin and suggested, ''If Brett gets a big hit in this series, let's ask to check his bat.''

It wouldn't have been the first time. In 1975, Thurman Munson singled in a run against Minnesota, but was called out when manager Frank Quillici noticed too much pine tar on his bat. The same year, John Mayberry of the Royals was involved in a pine-tar dispute. In fact, Royals manager Dick Howser had been warned by umpires about Brett's bat, but for one reason or another nothing was done about the sticky stuff.

On July 24, the Yanks and Royals were in the thick of pennant races when they met at Yankee Stadium. It was a crucial game and a crucial moment—ninth inning, Royals down 4–3 with two out and U. L. Washington on base. Brett, one of the best hitters in the game, stepped up and crushed a 1–0 fastball from Goose Gossage into the right-field bleachers.

Billy Martin, always a stickler for the rules when they worked to his advantage, calmly strolled out of the Yankee dugout and informed the umpires that Brett had been using an illegal bat because the pine tar extended too far up the handle. Billy pointed out good old Rule 6.06d, which states that a man is both called out and ejected from the game for hitting an illegally batted ball.

Lacking a ruler, plate umpire Tim McClelland placed the bat across home plate, which measures seventeen inches across, and saw that the pine tar extended far beyond the eighteen-inch limit (in fact, it was twenty-four inches). The umpires gathered to discuss the problem, and while Brett was still being thumped on the back by his teammates, a ruling was made: the bat was indeed illegal, the home run nullified, Brett was out, the game was over, and the Yankees had won.

"It didn't seem right to take away Brett's homer because of a little pine tar," said umpire Joe Brinkman. "But rules are rules. Rules are all an umpire has to work with."

Brett, one of baseball's more popular and respected players, became a crazy person, charged out of the dugout, and literally attacked McClelland. "He was a madman," said Brinkman, who was forced to grab the frenzied third baseman in a head-lock. "I can still see his bulging eyes and red face." (Brett was never punished for attacking the umpires, and later Billy Martin cracked, "If it had been *me*, they would have opened up Alcatraz.")

In all the confusion, Royals pitcher Gaylord Perry (who knows a thing or two about hiding foreign substances), grabbed the bat and began passing the evidence toward the Royals clubhouse. Brinkman chased it down and snatched it back.

That was only the beginning of the controversy. The Royals immediately filed a protest with American League president Lee MacPhail. Teams file protests all the time, and nothing much ever comes of them. MacPhail had been in office for ten years and had yet to uphold a single protest.

Surprise! Five days later, he ruled that the home run stood, that the score of the game was now 5–4 in favor of Kansas City, and that the game would be completed at a later date. MacPhail issued the following statement:

"It is the position of this office that the umpires' interpretation, while technically defensible, is not in accord with the intent or spirit of the rules and that the rules do not provide that a hitter be called out for excessive use of pine tar. Although manager Martin and his staff should be commended for their alertness, it is the strong conviction of the league that games should be won and lost on the playing field. The use of pine tar in itself shall not be considered doctoring the bat."

MacPhail was immediately blasted from all sides. For one thing, excessive use of pine tar *could* be considered doctoring a bat. It could be used to deaden bunts or to make the bat harder than ordinary wood. George Steinbrenner pointed out that people in Florida paint their fences with pine tar to harden the wood.

More important, if an umpire's decision based on a clearly stated rule is overturned, what does that say about abiding by rules and umpires? "They might as well burn the rule book," said pitching coach Sammy Ellis. "What Lee MacPhail has done," Billy Martin claimed, "is tell every kid in the country that they should go ahead and use illegal bats and cheat, and they can get away with it." "It may be a chickenshit rule," Graig Nettles plainly stated, "but it's a rule."

Baseball fan and former senator Eugene McCarthy summed up the position more eloquently in *The New Republic:* "The rules of baseball are not guidelines to be interpreted in the light of situational ethics. They are rules, and they are clear.... A batter who bats the ball with an illegal bat is to be called out."

McCarthy further speculated on the implications of Mac-Phail's decision. If it can be assumed that Brett would have hit his home run even *without* the pine tar, he said, it might also be ruled that a runner who tags up before a fly ball is caught should not be called out, because chances are he would have beaten the throw even if he had waited.

Billy Martin astutely pointed out that failure to touch a base is an offense similar to using too much pine tar. Both are usually technicalities, not intentional deceptions to gain an edge. But when a runner misses third base and the other team spots it, he doesn't get a "pardon" from the league president.

The Yankees did everything they could to sabotage the completion of the disputed game. Celebrity lawyer Roy Cohn was hired to argue the case in New York State Supreme Court. The players discussed not showing up for the game and simply taking a forfeit in protest.

When they finally took the field to resume the game, Martin put on an appeal play at every base, claiming that the new crew of umpires could not possibly know that Brett and Washington had touched all the bases. The umpires, having planned for such a ploy, produced an affidavit signed by the previous umpires attesting to the fact that both Brett and Washington tagged all the bases.

When the game resumed at last, the five hundred fans who came out to Yankee Stadium got to see twelve minutes of baseball. The Yankees didn't score with their remaining three outs, and the game was finally over—twenty-five days after it had begun.

After all was said and done, both teams fell out of pennant contention. The pine-tar episode had made the front page of the otherwise staid *New York Times*. The Hall of Fame requested the bat, and Brett was offered twenty thousand dollars for it by a private collector. (For the record, the bat is a Hillerich & Bradsby T-85, and the T stands for Marv Throneberry.) The rule book was changed, requiring complaints about illegal bats to be made *before* their use, not after.

Perhaps the irony of the entire incident is that George Brett's pine tar was supplied by the Yankees, as a courtesy to the visiting team.

The Super Ball Incident: September 7, 1974

The two most famous bat-cheating incidents in baseball history are linked by one man—Graig Nettles. He spotted the pine-tar overload on George Brett's bat, and he was *caught* using an illegal bat himself nine years earlier.

Nettles was having a good day against the Tigers on September 7, 1974. He hit a home run in the first game of the doubleheader and another in the second inning of the second game. This good fortune ended in the fifth inning, when Nettles slashed an opposite-field single to left. His bat split open upon impact, and had obviously been hollowed out. The interesting thing is that it wasn't corked, Styrofoamed, or sawdusted—it was Super Balled. Six little balls bounced out as Nettles was running to first. Catcher Bill Freehan picked up what was left of the bat and showed it to plate umpire Lou DiMuro.

"As soon as the end came off, I knew there was something wrong with it," said Nettles, who innocently claimed the bat had been given to him by a Yankee fan in Chicago. "I didn't know there was anything in the bat; that was the first time I used it."

Some mystery has grown up around this episode. Several accounts of it mention the Super Balls bouncing all over the infield, while others say the bat was merely corked. *The New York Times'* description of the game the next day doesn't say anything about balls. In his own book (conveniently titled *Balls*), Nettles writes, "There's a myth that little balls came flying out of the bat, but that never happened. Nothing came out."

Balls or no balls, the bat was declared illegal and Nettles was called out. The Yankees won anyway, 1–0, on the strength of the home run he had hit in the second inning.

Time magazine had the best line on the incident: "Nettles was the first man to bounce out to the third baseman, the shortstop, and the second baseman all at once."

The Year of the Cheater: 1987

On the morning of August 7, 1987, a very special patient was rushed to Executive Health Examiners at the corner of Third Avenue and 48th Street in Manhattan. Five officials nervously carried this patient up to the twenty-first floor of the imposing black office building for emergency X rays. When the film had been processed, the radiologists breathed a sigh of relief. The five officials breathed a sigh of relief. But more than anyone else, the New York Mets management breathed a sigh of relief. The X rays were negative. Third baseman Howard Johnson's bat was indeed a solid piece of wood.

In the year of Iranscam, a pot-smoking Supreme Court nominee, and a philandering evangelist, all-American baseball finally lost its wholesome-as-Mom-and-apple-pie image. A veritable crime wave gripped the sport that summer, and for the first time in one hundred years the commissioner's office stopped winking at illegal bats and balls. The cheaters of '87 made Gaylord Perry look like Mother Teresa.

On April 15, the Dodgers sent National League officials a dozen baseballs they claimed had been scuffed by Houston pitcher Mike Scott, after he had beaten them in a one-hitter. On June 23, umpires collected seven balls allegedly scuffed by Rick Rhoden. On July 5, after pitching against Scott, Phillies pitcher Kevin Gross said balls left behind by Scott at the end of each inning had marks on them.

On July 30, Cardinals manager Whitey Herzog claimed Howard Johnson of the Mets was a bat corker, and tried to grab Hojo's bat after a home run. Four days later, Joe Niekro was nabbed on the mound with an emery board and a piece of sandpaper contoured to the shape of his finger. Three days after that, Howard Johnson's bat was confiscated by the Cubs. After having accused Mike Scott of cheating, Kevin Gross was caught with a sticky substance and a piece of sandpaper glued in the pocket of his glove on August 10. "It was just there," explained Gross.

A week later, San Francisco Giant Candy Maldonado and Howard Johnson had their bats confiscated in the same game (Johnson led the league in X rays). Five days later, Don Sutton was filmed rubbing a ball with a mysterious strip on the palm of his hand. Finally, on September 1, Houston's Billy Hatcher took a swing and the barrel of his bat split open, spraying a rain of cork over the Astrodome infield.

By season's end, managers were allowed to have one opposing bat confiscated per game. Half the players in the majors were suspected of cheating. Niekro, Gross, and Hatcher were slapped with ten-day suspensions. (Niekro used the time off to appear on "Late Night with David Letterman" with a carpenter's apron, Vaseline, shoe polish, and a power sander. He also wrote a book with his brother Phil punningly titled *The Niekro Files*.)

There was talk of installing airport metal detectors in the on-deck circles, and replacing baseball bubble-gum cards with wanted posters. Jokes circulated about random bat testing with each random urine test, cork-sniffing dogs, and umpires reading the *Miranda* rule right after the national anthem.

It was a summer to remember. Many more will surely follow.

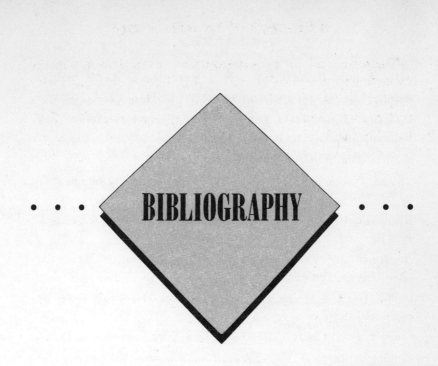

BIBLIOGRAPHY

Although baseball people are somewhat reluctant to discuss the topic of cheating, much has appeared in print. I gratefully acknowledge the valuable information gathered from the following sources.

Periodicals:

American Heritage Magazine, The American Journal of Physics, Baseball Digest, Baseball Magazine, Christian Century, Collier's, Fortune, Life, Literary Digest, Look, The New Republic, Newsweek, The New York Times, People, Popular Mechanics, Saturday Evening Post, Science Digest, Spalding's Official Baseball Guide, Sport, Sporting News, Sports Illustrated, Time.

Books:

Alexander, Charles C. *Ty Cobb* (New York: Oxford University Press, 1984).

· Bibliography ·

Allen, Maury. *Damn Yankee* (New York: Times Books, 1980).

Asinof, Eliot. *Eight Men Out* (New York: Henry Holt, 1963).

Boswell, Thomas. *How Life Imitates the World Series* (New York: Penguin, 1982).

Bouton, Jim. *Ball Four* (New York: Dell, 1970).

Braine, Tim, and John Stravinsky. *The Not So Great Moments in Sports* (New York: Morrow, 1986).

Brancazio, Peter J. *Sport Science* (New York: Simon & Schuster, 1984).

Brinkman, Joe. *The Umpire's Handbook* (Lexington, Mass.: Stephen Greene, 1985).

Carter, Gary. *A Dream Season* (New York: Harcourt Brace Jovanovich, 1987).

Chieger, Bob. *Voices of Baseball* (New York: Atheneum, 1983).

Connor, Anthony J. *Voices from Cooperstown* (New York: Macmillan, 1982).

Creamer, Robert W. *Stengel: His Life and Times* (New York: Simon & Schuster, 1984).

Dark, Alvin, and John Underwood. *When in Doubt, Fire the Manager* (New York: Dutton, 1980).

Durso, Joseph. *The Days of Mr. McGraw* (Englewood Cliffs, N.J.: Prentice-Hall, 1969).

Dykstra, Lenny. *Nails* (New York: Doubleday, 1987).

Eskenazi, Gerald. *Bill Veeck: A Baseball Legend* (New York: McGraw-Hill, 1988).

Frick, Ford. *Games, Asterisks and People* (New York: Crown, 1973).

Garagiola, Joe. *It's Anybody's Ballgame* (Chicago: Contemporary, 1988).

Hernandez, Keith. *If at First* (New York: Penguin, 1986).

Honig, Donald. *Baseball America* (New York: Macmillan, 1985).

Hornsby, Rogers, and Bill Surface. *My War with Baseball* (New York: Coward-McCann, 1962).

Hunter, Catfish. *Catfish* (New York: McGraw-Hill, 1988).

Johnson, Davey. *Bats* (New York: Putnam, 1986).

Johnstone, Jay. *Temporary Insanity* (Chicago: Contemporary Books, 1985).

Kuhn, Bowie. *Hardball* (New York: Random House, 1987).

Lardner, Ring. *The Portable Ring Lardner* (New York: Viking, 1946).

Lee, Bill. *The Wrong Stuff* (New York: Viking Penguin, 1984).

Levine, Peter. *A. G. Spalding and the Rise of Baseball* (New York: Oxford University Press, 1985).

Luciano, Ron. *Remembrance of Swings Past* (New York: Bantam, 1988).

Lyle, Sparky. *The Bronx Zoo* (New York: Crown, 1979).

McCarver, Tim. *Oh Baby I Love It!* (New York: Villard, 1987).

Mantle, Mickey. *The Mick* (New York: Doubleday, 1985).

Mays, Willie. *Say Hey* (New York: Simon & Schuster, 1988).

Nash, Bruce, and Allan Zullo. *Baseball Confidential* (New York: Simon & Schuster, 1988).

———. *The Baseball Hall of Shame,* 3 vols. (New York: Simon & Schuster, 1985–1987).

Nelson, Kevin. *Baseball's Greatest Insults* (New York: Simon & Schuster, 1984).

———. *Baseball's Greatest Quotes* (New York: Simon & Schuster, 1982).

Nettles, Graig, and Peter Golenbock. *Balls* (New York: Putnam, 1984).

Niekro, Phil and Joe. *The Niekro Files* (Chicago: Contemporary, 1988).

Palmer, Murray. *Branch Rickey* (New York: Atheneum, 1982).

Piersall, Jimmy. *The Truth Hurts* (Chicago: Contemporary, 1984).

Quigley, Martin. *The Crooked Pitch: The Curveball in American*

· Bibliography ·

Baseball History (Chapel Hill, N.C.: Algonquin Books, 1984).

Ritter, Lawrence. *The Glory of Their Times* (New York: Random House, 1966).

Ritter, Lawrence, and Donald Honig. *The Image of Their Greatness* (New York: Crown, 1979).

Robinson, Frank. *Extra Innings* (New York: McGraw-Hill, 1988).

Rogosin, Donn. *Invisible Men: Life in Baseball's Negro Leagues* (New York: Atheneum, 1987).

Schrier, Eric W., and William F. Allman. *Newton at the Bat* (New York: Scribner's, 1984).

Smith, Ozzie. *Wizard* (Chicago: Contemporary, 1988).

Snider, Duke. *The Duke of Flatbush* (New York: Zebra, 1988).

Thorn, John, and John Holway. *The Pitcher* (Englewood Cliffs, N.J.: Prentice-Hall, 1987).

Uecker, Bob. *Catcher in the Wry* (New York: Putnam, 1982).

Vincent, Ted. *Mudville's Revenge* (New York: Seaview Books, 1981).

Voigt, David Quentin. *American Baseball*, 2 vols. (Norman: University of Oklahoma Press, 1966, 1970).

Waggoner, Glen, Kathleen Moloney, and Hugh Howard. *Baseball by the Rules* (Taylor, 1987).

Weaver, Earl. *It's What You Learn After You Know It All That Counts* (New York: Simon & Schuster, 1982).

Winfield, Dave. *Winfield: A Player's Life* (New York: Norton, 1988).

FOR THE BEST IN PAPERBACKS, LOOK FOR THE Ⓟ

In every corner of the world, on every subject under the sun, Penguin represents quality and variety—the very best in publishing today.

For complete information about books available from Penguin—including Pelicans, Puffins, Peregrines, and Penguin Classics—and how to order them, write to us at the appropriate address below. Please note that for copyright reasons the selection of books varies from country to country.

In the United Kingdom: For a complete list of books available from Penguin in the U.K., please write to *Dept E.P., Penguin Books Ltd, Harmondsworth, Middlesex, UB7 0DA.*

In the United States: For a complete list of books available from Penguin in the U.S., please write to *Dept BA, Penguin,* Box 120, Bergenfield, New Jersey 07621-0120.

In Canada: For a complete list of books available from Penguin in Canada, please write to *Penguin Books Ltd, 2801 John Street, Markham, Ontario L3R 1B4.*

In Australia: For a complete list of books available from Penguin in Australia, please write to the *Marketing Department, Penguin Books Ltd, P.O. Box 257, Ringwood, Victoria 3134.*

In New Zealand: For a complete list of books available from Penguin in New Zealand, please write to the *Marketing Department, Penguin Books (NZ) Ltd, Private Bag, Takapuna, Auckland 9.*

In India: For a complete list of books available from Penguin, please write to *Penguin Overseas Ltd, 706 Eros Apartments, 56 Nehru Place, New Delhi, 110019.*

In Holland: For a complete list of books available from Penguin in Holland, please write to *Penguin Books Nederland B.V., Postbus 195, NL-1380AD Weesp, Netherlands.*

In Germany: For a complete list of books available from Penguin, please write to *Penguin Books Ltd, Friedrichstrasse 10-12, D-6000 Frankfurt Main 1, Federal Republic of Germany.*

In Spain: For a complete list of books available from Penguin in Spain, please write to *Longman, Penguin España, Calle San Nicolas 15, E-28013 Madrid, Spain.*

In Japan: For a complete list of books available from Penguin in Japan, please write to *Longman Penguin Japan Co Ltd, Yamaguchi Building, 2-12-9 Kanda Jimbocho, Chiyoda-Ku, Tokyo 101, Japan.*